# C.S.S. *SHENANDOAH*

*C.S.S. Shenandoah* (1865)

# C.S.S.
# *SHENANDOAH*

## *The Memoirs of*

## *Lieutenant Commanding James I. Waddell*

EDITED BY

# JAMES D. HORAN

NAVAL INSTITUTE PRESS

ANNAPOLIS, MARYLAND

BLUEJACKET BOOKS

*For our Gary*

Published by arrangement with Crown Publishers, Inc.
First Bluejacket Books printing, 1996

Library of Congress Cataloging-in-Publication Data


Waddell, James I. (James Iredell), 1824–1886.
C.S.S. Shenandoah : the memoirs of Lieutenant Commanding James
I. Waddell / editied by James D. Horan.
p.    cm. — (Bluejacket books)
Originally published: New York : Crown Publishers, [1960].
Includes bibliographical references.
ISBN 1-55750-368-0 (pbk. : alk. paper)
1. Waddell, James I. (James Iredell), 1824–1886.   2. Shenandoah
(Cruiser)   3. United States—History—Civil War, 1861–1865—Personal
narratives, Confederate.   4. United States—History—Civil War,
1861–1865—Naval operations.   5. Ship captains—Confederate States
of America—Biography.   I. Horan, James David, 1914–   .
II. Title.   III. Series.
E599.S5W3   1996
973.7′57′092—dc20
[B]                                                                           95-38811


Printed in the United States of America on acid-free paper ∞

03 02 01 00 99 98 97 96   8 7 6 5 4 3 2 1

# Contents

# Acknowledgments

For the assistance so generously and unfailingly given him in the accumulation of material for this book, the author is deeply grateful to:

Patrick C. Courtney, Secretary-Treasurer of the Confederate Research Club of England
Thomas Green, Hampshire, England
Chris Svendsen, Seamen's Institute
Jim Dan Hill, State College, Superior, Wisconsin
William Deane, Liverpool, England
Richard G. Wood, War Records, National Archives
Norma Cuthbert, Department of Manuscripts, Henry E. Huntington Library and Art Gallery, San Marino, California
Samuel G. Kelly, Captain (ret.), Asst. Director Naval History, Department of the Navy
David C. Mearns, Chief, Manuscript Division, Library of Congress
Mabel C. Weaks, Archivist, Filson Club, Louisville, Kentucky
R. O'Hare, Schenectady, New York
Tom Baab, Seamen's Institute
William C. Brinkley, *Mississippi Valley Historical Review*
D. L. Corbitt, *North Carolina Historical Review*
J. W. Dudley, Assistant Archivist Virginia State Library
James C. Olson, Mississippi Valley Historical Society
A. J. Motley, Chicago Historical Society
H. W. Johnson, Public Records Office, London, England
Wayne Andrews, formerly New York Historical Society
Sylvester Vigilante, New York Historical Society
Nelson W. Blake, War Records, National Archives
Mrs. Theodore Douglas Robinson, Mohawk, New York
E. M. Eller, Rear Admiral (ret.), Director Naval History, Dept. of the Navy
John B. Heffernan, Rear Admiral (ret.), Director Naval History, Dept. of the Navy

# A Prefatory Note about the
# C.S.S. Shenandoah and
# Other Confederate Cruisers

The last shot of the Civil War was fired, not on an obscure battlefield, but in the ice-locked Sea of Okhotsk off Siberia seven months after Lee's surrender.

The last armed Confederate cruiser was the C.S.S. *Shenandoah*, a beautiful but dangerous vessel which scattered and burned the New Bedford whaling fleet in Arctic waters. She was the last cruiser sent to sea by James Dunwoody Bulloch, the captain who built the Confederacy's navy in the shipyards of Europe.

Constructed at a cost of £53,715, the *Shenandoah* captured thirty-eight ships and burned thirty-two. She inflicted damage to Union commerce which was officially judged at $1,361,983. She took 1,053 prisoners. In fact, she took so many her skipper, Lieutenant-Commanding James Waddell, had to rig a chain of whaleboats that could be towed along by his vessel, to accommodate captured Union seamen and the crews of the whalers he had burned.

A few years after the war, Waddell wrote his account of the *Shenandoah*'s great cruise, and it is published here complete for the first time. He tells of his own career in the United States Navy and in the Confederate Navy, and also of the events leading up to his taking command of the *Shenandoah*.

But to give the *Shenandoah*'s story its proper historical

Captain James D. Bulloch
Confederate States Navy Agent in England

2

perspective, it must be linked with Bulloch, his activities as the Confederate Naval Agent in Europe, and the cruisers and tenders he built and purchased.

Bulloch was sent to Europe early in 1861, after the leaders of the newborn Confederate States of America realized that the weakest link in their military program lay not on land but on the sea. They knew the South did not have a navy to challenge Union control of the sea, and without warships, the Confederacy would be unable to acquire supplies and material from abroad. The Union armies, on the other hand, could draw on the economic resources of the entire world.

There were no extensive shipyards or shipbuilding facilities in the South, but there were in England and in France. It was on the stocks and ways of Liverpool and Calais that the leaders of the Confederacy envisioned a mighty fleet of warships and raiders.[1]

Bulloch was a member of a Georgian family that had played a long and distinguished role in American politics and nautical affairs. His grandfather had been the Revolutionary governor of Georgia. His father, James Stephens Bulloch, was a member of that distinguished company of Americans who planned and sponsored the *Savannah*'s famous voyage from Savannah to Liverpool. His mother was Hester Amerinthea, daughter of Senator John Elliott.

James Dunwoody Bulloch was born near Savannah, June 10, 1823. Most of his formative years were spent at "Bulloch Hall," Roswell, not far from Atlanta. From as early as he could remember, Bulloch wanted to follow the sea.[2] At

[1] William P. Roberts, "James Dunwoody Bulloch and the Confederate Navy," *The North Carolina Historical Review*, pp. 315-366. This is an excellent account of Bulloch's career in England.

[2] L. L. Knight, *Georgia's Landmarks, Memorials and Legends*, Vol. II, p. 217 (hereinafter cited as Knight).

sixteen he entered the United States Navy. After fourteen years of honorable service on many ships of the line, he left the Navy to enter the Merchant Marine. One of his commands was the *Black Warrior,* a merchantship famous in her time, which played a stirring role in the diplomatic history of the United States when she was seized by Spanish authorities in Cuba. The international negotiations resulting from her seizure led to the famous Ostend Manifesto.[3]

On January 11, 1861, Georgia seceded from the Union. Bulloch at the time was commanding the mail steamer *Bienville.* A man of deep integrity, he immediately returned the ship to its New York owners. After docking her at Canal Street, he paid a brief visit at the home of his New York relatives, the Roosevelts. There a solemn-eyed child listened to his elders talking of the growing crisis. Years later, in the White House, President Theodore Roosevelt would recall the visit of his "Uncle James."

Bulloch had many friends in northern shipping circles. He says in his memoirs, "I had no property of any kind in the South, nor any pecuniary interest of any kind in that part of the country." As the war clouds thickened, he waited, hoping that the North and South would heal their differences.

But in the early hours of dawn, April 13, 1861, Beauregard ordered the firing on Fort Sumter, and the war was on. That same day Bulloch wrote to his friend Judah P. Benjamin, then the Confederacy's Attorney General, offering his services to his beloved South.

Three weeks later, the South's Secretary of the Navy,

---

[3] J. D. Bulloch, *The Secret Service of the Confederate States in Europe, or, How the Confederate Cruisers Were Equipped,* Vol. 1, p. 32 (hereinafter cited as Bulloch).

Stephen P. Mallory, ordered Bulloch to go abroad to secure ships and supplies, to build a Confederate navy, particularly warships that could prey on Union shipping. Mallory directed Bulloch to be "prudent and heedful" and not to involve the Confederacy's diplomatic agents in any embarrassing incidents. He gave the 38-year-old Bulloch an order for several steam-propelled vessels which could be used as raiders. Since it was important that the Confederacy have vessels at sea immediately, Mallory suggested that Bulloch at first purchase ships already built, and then give his whole attention to the construction of cruisers.

Mallory's description of the ships he wanted "immediately" is typically bureaucratic: "The type of ships desired for immediate use is that which offers the greatest chance for success against the enemy's commerce."[4]

On the evening of May 9, 1861, Bulloch left Montgomery to sail for Europe. His assignment as a Confederate agent was to be one of the most important and most arduous of the entire Civil War. The Confederacy had only one fighting ship, the *Sumter*. Southern shipbuilding was confined to Norfolk and Pensacola, and these facilities could not produce fighting ships. Therefore Bulloch was faced with building an entire wartime navy in foreign ports. In addition, he was to purchase and somehow send back all types of military supplies.

The obstacles Bulloch faced were tremendous: The South had no hard cash—only cotton. The diplomatic fences which confronted her ministers were almost impossible to hurdle.[5]

[4] *Official Records of the Union and Confederate Navies in the War of Rebellion*, Second Series, p. 64 (hereinafter cited as OR).

[5] D. Jourdan and J. C. Pratt, *Europe and the American Civil War*, pp. 10-12. An excellent book dealing with the diplomatic hurdles Bulloch faced in building the Confederate Navy in England and France.

For example, Jefferson Davis sent William Lowden Yancey, Pierre A. Rost, and A. Dudley Mann to England, but Lord Palmerston's government refused to receive them.

In England, the Confederacy was opposed by one of its greatest foes. President Lincoln had appointed Charles Francis Adams, son of John Quincy Adams and grandson of John Adams, to the post at St. James. Although Adams appeared a "cold codfish" to his overworked secretary, Benjamin Moran, he was one of the most efficient diplomats in the history of the State Department.

Bulloch was also faced with an efficient United States consul in Liverpool, Thomas H. Dudley. Dudley had neither the cultural background nor the poise of Adams, but he had unlimited energy, a fierce patriotism, and a deep hatred for the Confederacy. The cold, aloof, Bostonian Adams and the energetic Liverpool consul proved to be an almost unbeatable diplomatic team. Bulloch and his agents would defeat them from time to time, but in winning the battles and skirmishes, they would completely lose the war.

When Bulloch arrived in England, Her Majesty's government did not have a clearly defined doctrine in international law that spelled out the obligations of a neutral nation relative to constructing and fitting out armed vessels for a belligerent state. Even the domestic laws of Great Britain were hazy on whether building cruisers constituted an unneutral act for British subjects.

The Union's principal weapon was England's Foreign Enlistment Act of 1819, which, among other things, forbade English subjects to "equip, furnish, fit out or arm" a ship that would be used against a nation "with which His Majesty shall not then be at war." The Act also made it unlawful to place an order or deliver such an order to fit out or arm a vessel for the same purposes. Violators were to be fined and the ship seized by the government.

The unpopular law was ambiguous, and its ambiguity had not been removed by judicial interpretation. In fact, only one minor case had been tried under the Act when the Civil War began.

The British government was slow to bring charges against alleged violators of the Act for fear that Her Majesty's government would be assessed damages in case the higher courts ruled against the Queen's Solicitor. In addition, Victoria's representatives bluntly told the United States representatives that the burden of proof would be on them if they initiated the charges. This view embittered Adams and Dudley, who felt they were being asked not only to enforce England's own law but also to seek out, and provide in court, evidence that would stand a legal test.[6]

In France, also, Bulloch's shipbuilding plans ran into a good deal of difficulty, for the spring of 1861 saw Napoleon III publishing a proclamation of neutrality. However, Slidell, that suave onetime Tammany politician, did make some headway. He could play cards with Drouin de Lhuys, French foreign minister, and be received by Napoleon, but he could never get the Emperor to move either diplomatically or militarily. Like Bulloch, Slidell was opposed by a shrewd and knowing United States consul, John Bigelow, that "forgotten patriot." Bigelow outguessed, outfought, and outmaneuvered Bulloch, Slidell, and their agents.[7]

This was the situation in which Bulloch found himself

[6] Douglas H. Maynard, "Union Attempts to Prevent the Escape of the Alabama," *The Mississippi Valley Historical Review*, June, 1954, p. 43.
[7] Burton J. Hendrick, *Statesmen of the Lost Cause*, pp. 222, 283.

Mathew Brady's picture of John Bigelow. *From Mathew Brady: Historian with a Camera.*

when he stepped ashore in England on June 4, 1861. Because of the very nature of his role as a Confederate agent, he did not wear a uniform. After calling upon the Confederate commissioners, Yancy, Rost, and Mann, he turned to Fraser, Trenholm and Company, the financial lights of the Confederacy. Here he met Charles K. Prioleau, variously described as a resident manager and partner of the company. Although Bulloch would deal with the other members of the company, he worked closely with Prioleau until the end of the war. After their first meeting, Bulloch established his headquarters in that company.[8]

The plan to buy already completed ships at once hit a snag; Bulloch found there were no ships for sale. With Prioleau underwriting the orders, he then contracted with Fawcett, Preston and Company, a Liverpool firm, to build a wooden ship 185 feet in length, designed along the lines of a British gunboat. She was to be equipped with heavy fire power and be completed by December, 1861, at the cost of £45,628.[9] Originally named the *Oreto*, later rechristened the C.S.S. *Florida*, she became the first member of the Confederacy's overseas navy.

While the *Florida's* gun mounts were being laid, Bulloch turned to Lairds' shipyards at Brinkenham, across the Mersey River from Liverpool, to build his next vessel. This time he worked very closely with the designers, incorporating many of his own ideas. When the keel was laid, it was given the number 290; this vessel became the famous *Alabama*.[10]

With the workmen swarming about the scaffolding of the

[8] Fraser, Trenholm and Company was the Liverpool branch of the Charleston banking firm of John Fraser and Company. The president of the firm was George A. Trenholm.
[9] Bulloch to Mallory, Aug. 13, 1861. OR, Series I, p. 95.
[10] Bulloch to Mallory, Aug. 13, 1861. OR, Second Series, p. 65.

C.S.S. *Florida*

C.S.S. *Stonewall*. Constructed in France, this was the only ram that ever got to sea under the Confederate colors.

Lairds' shipyards on the Mersey as they appeared in the early 1860's.

11

290, toiling at night under torches, Bulloch could turn his attention to the purchase of supplies. Working with Huse and Anderson, the two Confederate agents for the army, he obtained a large amount—guns, powder, food, and medicine—but the problem was to get them across the ocean, past the blockade, and into the Confederacy.

Bulloch quietly purchased a steamer called the *Fingal* for £17,500 and loaded it to the gunwales with supplies. Rather than give the responsibility to another man, he took command of the ship himself and sailed it to Savannah, not only demonstrating that the blockade was ineffective, but establishing a record that was never equaled during the war. No other ship ever delivered to the Confederacy a cargo so completely military.[11]

Bulloch stayed in the South five months before he again slipped through the blockade on a fast moon-chaser for Liverpool.

To get the *Florida* to sea now occupied all Bulloch's attention. He renamed her the *Palermo* and had her registered in the name of an Italian merchant with offices in Liverpool. He got her past Adams' agents and armed her at a rendezvous in the Caribbean. At Nassau she was turned over to Captain James N. Maffit and rechristened the *Florida,* and from there she set out on a voyage that was to result in the sinking and capturing of many Union ships.

Bulloch's most fervent desire was that he be made captain of a cruiser, and he made his wish clear to Richmond a few months after he had arrived in England.[12]

In the winter of 1862 he was made a commander and assigned to the first ship to leave England. There was, how-

[11] Bulloch's obituary in *The Confederate Veteran* IX (1901).
[12] Bulloch to Mallory, November 13, 1861. OR, Second Series, pp. 86-87.

12

C.S.S. *Alabama*

ever, a great deal of professional jealousy among the Confederate flag officers, and soon after the news got out, Lieutenant James H. North, who was building ships in Glasgow under Bulloch's direction, protested to Mallory. North's ruffled feathers were smoothed when he was raised in rank some months later; Bulloch, meanwhile, was given his choice of a ship to command.

Ironically, fine seaman that he was, Bulloch never did have an opportunity to make a choice; he never attained command. Semmes was given command of the 290, christened first the *Enrica* by a pretty but unknown young lady, then the *Alabama;* she became one of the great sea raiders of the war. Bulloch was bitter, but he bowed to the judgment of his superiors in Richmond. In this instance they were correct; there were plenty of able seamen, but not many with Bulloch's ability to organize a complex shipbuilding program, maintain his own counterintelligence unit, fight English bureaucracy and red tape, and stand toe to toe with Adams and Dudley in the formal but relentless ring of international wartime diplomacy.

Bulloch finally got the *Alabama* to sea in the false guise of a "builder's run," aided by the illness of one of Her Majesty's personnel.[13] Not only did the cruiser inflict tremendous damage on American shipping; the "sickness" of one of England's clerks cost that nation $15,000,000.[14]

The *Florida* and *Alabama,* for all their swift, hawklike sea attacks, were only wooden ships and were far from powerful enough to attack Union warships. This Mallory realized

[13] Brooks Adams, "The Seizure of the Laird Rams," *Proceedings of the Massachusetts Historical Society."* XLV (1911-1912), p. 290.

[14] Price Edwards, Customs Collector at Liverpool, was charged with bribery in allowing the *Alabama* to get to sea, but Bulloch later denied this charge.

14

Heretofore unpublished photographs of H.M.S. *Scorpion* (above) and H.M.S. *Wivern*, originally Confederate rams, constructed on contract placed by Commander Bulloch. The *Wivern* was launched August 29, 1863. Her specifications—"Iron ship, two turrets, one funnel, three masts (tripod), 220 feet long, 42 feet beam, 17 foot draught. Displacement 2750 tons. Armour: Four 9 inch 12½ ton muzzle loading guns, two in each turret."

from the lesson taught by the first Confederate ironclad, which had been built on the superstructure of the *Merrimac*. It sank two of the Union warships on blockade duty, the *Cumberland* and the *Congress*. Mallory sent word to Bulloch to get busy on ironclads at once.

The great dream was twenty-five iron rams, but Bulloch settled for two, built by Lairds'. One, the 294, was one of the most powerful warships in the world. Had she ever sailed under the Confederate flag, the outcome of the Civil War would have been changed. This is not only my opinion, but also that of Brooks Adams as stated in his article, "The Seizure of the Laird Rams."

The rams were to be 220 feet long, covered with a foot thickness of teak and railroad iron. Rigged as barks and fitted with steam, their calculated speed was to be 10½ knots. Their fire power was to be in two revolving turrets.

Adams and his diplomatic team put up a fierce battle, and Adams bluntly threatened England with war if they sailed. In the end, they were sold by Bulloch and became British naval warships, H.M.S. *Wivern* and H.M.S. *Scorpion*.[15]

Bulloch then turned to France to build his rams, but there he was stopped by John Bigelow, then United States Minister to France. Bigelow was able to circumvent Bulloch's plans through a young Frenchman, secretary to a shipbuilder in Calais, who sold his information to the Embassy. The young Judas simply walked into Bigelow's office one day and asked if he wanted to buy information about the rams, now near completion. Barely able to contain his excitement, Bigelow said he was in the market for such in-

[15] Bulloch, *Secret Service*, Vol. 1, p. 389.

formation, but had no intention of buying a pig in a poke.[16]

The informer then burglarized his employer's office at night, copied the incriminating evidence, and turned it over to Bigelow for payment. On such human frailties does the shape of history depend.

Despite the setbacks, in both England and France, to his program of building the powerful rams, Bulloch continued to buy ships. A study of the diplomatic correspondence of the Civil War shows that these included tenders fitted out to supply the needs of his ships already at sea. Among them were the *Hawk*, the *Louisa Ann Fanny*, the *Phantom*, and the *Southern*.

Although these were barely mentioned in letters and reports, they did not escape Adams' attention. Whenever he received a report from Liverpool, Adams would at once send a sharp note to Earl Russell demanding that England take action. However, there are no records that these supply ships were seized, and we can assume they went safely to sea.[17]

The raiders that Bulloch did get to sea inflicted enormous damage to Union commerce. Before the *Alabama* was sunk by the *Kearsarge*, her commander, Captain Semmes, reported that he had not been able to speak a Federal ship for three weeks. Even after the *Alabama* had been sunk, Federal shipping remained in port or sailed under neutral colors.

In 1864, with the Confederacy going downhill "with a downward pull," as realistic leaders in Richmond whispered

[16] John Bigelow, *France and the Confederate Navy*, p. 15. See also the Bigelow Papers, Manuscript Room, N. Y. Public Library, which contain Bigelow's secret messages.
[17] *Papers Relating to the Treaty of Washington*, Vol. I, p. 250.

17

among themselves, Bulloch and Mallory decided to step up their sea raids. Not only did they want to make sure that Union commerce was completely driven from the seven seas; they even elected to attack one of the North's most lucrative businesses—the New Bedford whaling fleet operating in the Pacific and Arctic oceans off Siberia.[18]

In the spring of 1864, Mallory was agreeing with Bulloch's plan of attack on the station, and he urged Bulloch to build or buy more cruisers "in the style of the *Alabama*."

Bulloch knew that Matthew Maguire, Dudley's detective, had infiltrated into Lairds' shipyards and it would be foolish to waste money in trying to build another cruiser. Although Bulloch's cash was now running low, English shipbuilders were making almost daily visits to his office, offering to build cruisers, the bills to be paid later with cotton. One builder offered to build six iron rams if the Confederacy signed a pledge to deliver cotton at eight cents a pound. But Bulloch had had enough of rams, and they never left the planning board.[19]

Bulloch was also supervising the buying of ships by other agents, particularly the scientist Matthew Fontaine Maury, who bought the iron screw steamer *Japan*, which became the C.S.S. *Georgia*. When the Royal Navy sold some of its ships, Bulloch's agents, through a dummy, bought the 500-ton screw steamer *Victor*. Dudley finally got wind of the sale, and Adams started diplomatic proceedings to have England seize her. Warned by his counter-agents, Bulloch ordered the ship to Calais in Christmas week, 1864. She became the C.S.S. *Rappahannock*. However, after a trial

[18] Mallory to Bulloch, March 12, 1864. OR, Second Series, p. 613.
[19] Bulloch, *Secret Service*, Vol. II, pp. 248-252.

18

There are about 50 men on board now, and more are expected on Monday.

(Reported Saturday July 26th 1862).

William Passmore heard last night, that the gunboat would haul into the river, and sail to-day (Tuesday July 29th 1862) on a trial trip and would not return again. Her crew have been paid a half month's advance on Monday July 28th.

(Reported Tuesday July 29th 1862).

On Friday July 18th 1862, two dozen of swords were taken on board the 290'ss. Sailed Tuesday, July 29th 1862 at 10 A. M. She has taken a crew (according to what the shipping master says) of between 90 and 100 men. The seamen signed articles to go to Nassau, Savannah or any other port or ports. They were told

The captain who is to take charge of her when she gets to Nassau told the seamen that he wanted men not cowards." One of the seamen asked him if they were going to run the blockade? the captain said he would let them know. The captain is a low sized, stoutish man, with black bushy whiskers, moustache and beard, apparently, a foreigner.

Excerpts from the heretofore unpublished reports of Matthew Maguire, secret agent for United States Consul Thomas Dudley, in Liverpool, and Charles Francis Adams, U.S. Minister to the Court of St. James. *Courtesy of Mrs. Theodore Douglas Robinson.*

run, he decided she was not strong enough to risk a battle with the Federal cruisers and ordered her sold.[20]

In the fall of 1864, Bulloch heard about the *Sea King*, "a long, rakish vessel of a registry of 790 tons with an auxiliary engine of 220 nominal horse power." She had been built in Glasgow by Stevens and Sons, one of the finest shipbuilders in the world. The year before, she had made one trip to Bombay as an army transport.[21]

Bulloch sent Richard Wright, son-in-law of Prioleau, to look the ship over. His eyes glowed when young Wright reported the *Sea King* was one of the fastest ships afloat; she had done 320 miles in twenty-five hours, and her engines had not showed any strain.[22]

But while Bulloch was hearing young Wright's report, Dudley was reporting to Adams that he had seen the *Sea King*, and she was "a likely steamer for the purposes of a privateer."[23]

During that fall of 1864, Richmond, desperately trying to ward off the inevitable defeat, was pouring hundreds of thousands of dollars into the Northwest Conspiracy engineered by Captain Thomas H. Hines, the bold Confederate agent. Throughout the North, Hines's men were making grand plans, but these somehow never came off. It was at this hour that Bulloch purchased the *Sea King* with the intention of using her as his weapon to destroy the New Bedford whaling fleet in the Pacific and the Arctic. She would be the last cruiser he would buy; she was the last hope of the Confederate Navy.

[20] Flag Officer Barron to Mallory, May, 1864. OR, Second Series, pp. 652-653.
[21] Bulloch to Waddell, Oct. 5, 1864. OR, First Series, p. 650.
[22] C. E. Hunt, *The Shenandoah or the Last Confederate Cruiser*, p. 90.
[23] Dudley to Seward and Morse to Seward. OR, Vol. VI.

Bulloch tried to make this sale airtight. He proceeded cautiously, telling his plans to only a trusted few. He sent Wright to Scotland and had him make the deal in his own name. Then he ordered the *Sea King* to several English ports, slipping her in and out in an attempt to make it appear she was an innocent merchantman.

On October 7, 1864, Wright gave power of attorney to Captain G. H. Corbett, a tough old sea dog who had commanded a blockade-runner Bulloch had purchased to ship army supplies to the South. Wright's written orders to Corbett were to sell the *King* "at any time within six months for the sum of not less than £45,000 sterling."[24]

Finally, on a clear and sparkling October morning in 1864, the beautiful *Sea King*, harbor trimmed, gaskets tight, and decks gleaming, raised her anchor and pointed her forefoot seaward. Dudley's detectives, watching her go down the channel through their spyglasses, noted she did not carry turret mounts on her decks nor was she sheathed with teak planking or railroad iron. Her only fire power was two twelve-pounders, "which was normal for an East India merchantman."[25]

In Bulloch's Liverpool offices the lamps burned late as he and his agents worked feverishly to make the *Sea King* one of the most formidable cruisers of the Confederate Navy. Bulloch had purchased a large supply ship, the *Laurel*, and had loaded her to the gunwales with guns, powder, and supplies. Aboard the *Laurel* were a number of Confederate officers and seamen, some of whom had seen service on the *Florida* and *Alabama*. Also aboard was the man Mallory had selected as captain of the new cruiser, Lieutenant Com-

[24] *Papers Relating to the Treaty of Washington,* Vol. I, p. 160.
[25] Hunt's *Shenandoah,* pp. 8-10.

manding James I. Waddell. Physically Waddell was a man of medium height, with black hair and thick sideburns. Years of service on the quarterdecks of many United States ships of the line had stained his face a deep mahogany. An old dueling wound made him limp slightly. He was very proud of his home state, and in later years would boast that he had been the only North Carolinian aboard the *Shenandoah.*

He was not a warm man; like Semmes of the *Alabama,* he had a tendency to remain aloof from both his crew and his officers. But he was a man of vast integrity, and he had an almost fanatical devotion to official orders. Before his ship's voyage ended, he would make a remarkable record as a seaman.

The *Laurel* left Liverpool at the same hour the *Sea King* left her coaling station on the Mersey. The destination of both ships was Funchal on the Island of Madeira. There they met eleven days later, and the transfer of supplies and guns took place.[26]

The *Laurel* arrived first. Two days later the *Sea King* hove to. The *Laurel*'s captain signaled the *Sea King* to round the Desertas, a barren, rocky island lying near Madeira, and proceed to the place of rendezvous.

> Tackles were at once got aloft on both vessels and they commenced operations by first transferring from the Laurel to the Sea King the heavy guns. At the expiration of thirty-six hours the transfer was effected, and the munitions of war, the clothing and stores with which the Laurel had been laden, were piled in utter confusion on the decks and in the hold of the Sea King which was to bear that name no longer.
>
> They took in from the Laurel, eight cannon, viz. six large and two small, with their carriages, (the guns were called 68 pounders) a quantity of powder, muskets, pistols, shot and

[26] Bulloch to Mallory, November 17, 1864. OR, Second Series, p. 757.

22

shell, clothing and a quantity of other stores, and also a quantity of coal.[27]

After the transfer of the supplies and guns had been completed, the Union Jack was lowered and the Stars and Bars of the Confederacy raised. In the warm sunshine Waddell officially took possession of the ship from Captain Corbett, and named her the C.S.S. *Shenandoah*. He made a rather stiff speech in which he asked the British crewmen to remain aboard and sign on. Some did, but at least ten refused, electing to return to England aboard the *Laurel*.

After the articles were signed and the main brace split, the *Laurel* pulled away. There were cheers and final good-bys as the *Shenandoah* swung out of the harbor to begin one of the most fantastic voyages in the annals of the sea.

In Liverpool and London, Adams was demanding that Great Britain take steps to seize the *Shenandoah*. But the ship was out to sea, and all Earl Russell could do was listen with elaborate patience to Adams' protests.

On November 18, 1864, Adams followed up his visits with a letter to Russell, summing up the United States' case against the Confederate States for having armed and fitted out the *Shenandoah* in English ports. The letter was typical of Adams, concise, factual, and blunt:

> These vessels (the Laurel and the Shenandoah) were at the time of their sailing, equipped and manned by English subjects; yet they were sent out with arms, ammunition, war supplies and officers and enlisted men for the purpose of initiating a hostile enterprise against the people of the United States against whom Britain at the time was under solemn obligation to preserve peace . . .[28]

[27] Hunt's *Shenandoah*, p. 14.
[28] *Alabama Claims Case of the United States*, p. 422.

| Hour | K. | F. | Courses. | Winds. | Lee Way. | At Sea    REMARKS.    Oct. 19th 1864 |
|---|---|---|---|---|---|---|
| 1 | | | | | | Having received everything from the |
| 2 | | | | | | Str Laurel at sea, put Ship in |
| 3 | | | | | | commission as C.S. Str. "Shenandoah" |
| 4 | | | | | | and shipped twenty three (23) men |
| 5 | | | | | | as Petty officers seamen, firemen, and |
| 6 | | | | | | coal heavers Weighed anchor at 2 oc P.M. |
| 7 | | | | | | and at 6 oc parted company with |
| 8 | | | | | | the Laurel when we hoised the Confd |
| 9 | | | | | | Ensign for the first time. 6.15 stood under |
| 10 | | | | | | steam to the SW. Pleasant weather and |
| 11 | | | | | | heavy swell from N.d. Wind N.E. |
| 12 | | | | | | |
| 1 | | | | | |            Irvine S. Bulloch |
| 2 | | | | | | From 8 to Midnight. |
| 3 | | | | | |            Set Fore and Main |
| 4 | | | | | | Topsails and at 9 oc let steam |
| 5 | | | | | | go down. |
| 6 | 3 | | Steby W | N.E. | |      (Signed) J. F. Minor |
| 7 | 7 | 2 | " | " | | |
| 8 | 2 | 2 | " | " | | |
| 9 | 2 | 2 | " | " | | |
| 10 | 2 | 2 | " | " | | |
| 11 | 2 | | " | " | | |
| 12 | | | | | | |

| Course | Dist. | Dif. Lat. | Dep. | Lat. by Acct. Barometer | Lat. by Obs. Sex. | Dif. Lon. Thermometer | Lon. by Acct. | Lon. by Obs. |
|---|---|---|---|---|---|---|---|---|
| | | | | | | | | |

24

| Hour | K. | F. | Courses | Winds | Lee Way | At Sea | REMARKS. 23d October |
|---|---|---|---|---|---|---|---|
| 1 | 10 | | NbW | EbNE | | | |
| 2 | 9 | | " | " | | | |
| 3 | 10 | | " | " | | | |
| 4 | 9 | 8 | " | " | | | Commences with strong winds |
| 5 | 9 | 8 | North | " | | | & squally. in royals, fly. jib |
| 6 | 8 | 8 | " | " | | | & topgallant staysails and |
| 7 | 8 | | NbE | SbyN | | | fore & mizzen topgallantsails |
| 8 | 8 | | " | " | | | Unbent Mn. royal & miz. T.G. |
| 9 | 10 | | NbW | " | | | staysails at Ryate & placed |
| 10 | 10 | | " | " | | | sail & co. & spanker. |
| 11 | 9 | 4 | " | " | | | Middle part |
| 12 | 9 | 4 | " | Var. | | | moderate breeze |
| 1 | 9 | 4 | NbW | " | | | & clear, in royals, flying jib |
| 2 | 9 | 4 | North | " | | | & main topgallant staysail |
| 3 | 9 | 4 | NbW | " | | | |
| 4 | 9 | 4 | North | " | | | Latter part |
| 5 | 10 | | " | " | | | Paling clouds |
| 6 | 10 | | NbE | " | | | and fresh trades. |
| 7 | 9 | 4 | North | " | | | |
| 8 | 9 | 4 | NbE | " | | | |
| 9 | 10 | | NbyE | SbyN | | | |
| 10 | 10 | | " | " | | | |
| 11 | 9 | 4 | North | EbNE | | | |
| 12 | 9 | | " | " | | | |

| Course | Dist. | Dif. Lat. | Dep. | Lat. by Acct. BAROMETER | Lat. by Obs. SEX. | Dif. Lon. THERMOMETER | Lon. by Acct. | Lon. by Obs. |
|---|---|---|---|---|---|---|---|---|
| NbyWbW | 214 miles. | | | | 25° 30' N | | | 34° 16' W. |

Two pages from the log of the *Shenandoah*. The first entry is signed by a nephew of James Dunwoody Bulloch, Confederate Navy Agent in Europe. *Courtesy of Chicago Historical Society.*

25

While the diplomatic wars continued in the drawing rooms of London, the *Shenandoah* swept into the South Atlantic to leave behind a string of burning ships, then around the Cape of Good Hope and to Australia, where Waddell ostensibly put in for repairs. In Melbourne, Captain Waddell discovered in United States Consul Blanchard another Dudley. The consul was at work an hour after the raider dropped anchor off Sandridge, a small town two miles from the city.

Reading Blanchard's reports to the Australian governor, one is impressed by the efficiency of his agents. In pinpointing the *Shenandoah* as the former *Sea King*, named in the letter sent by Dudley to all the United States consuls throughout the world some weeks before, Blanchard noted that his agents reported the "service plate" aboard the ship bore the name "Sea King."[29]

But Australia refused to act, pointing out that under international law she had to treat the *Shenandoah* as a warship belonging to a belligerent power. Then Blanchard charged Waddell's officers were "recruiting seamen right on the streets of the city."

In his memoirs Waddell does not mention Blanchard by name, nor does he disclose the real reason why he sailed to Australia. There is little doubt that the *Shenandoah* really needed repairs, but Blanchard's reports, letters, and investigations make it clear Waddell's officers obviously—and with his knowledge—were trying to recruit Australian seamen to fill out his small crew. Blanchard bombarded the Crown Solicitor with letters and the affidavits of seamen who had been approached by the *Shenandoah's* officers.

[29] *The Cases of the United States to be laid before the Tribunals of Arbitration to be convened at Geneva,* p. 425 (hereinafter cited as Tribunal).

At one point—and this Waddell dodges very neatly in his own account—Blanchard triumphantly presented evidence to the Governor that an Australian seaman named "Charley the Cook" and several companions had signed articles to ship aboard the *Shenandoah.*

The Australian Crown Solicitor began his investigation of the affidavits presented by Blanchard in the name of the United States by summoning Waddell and asking him if he were really hiding any Australian subjects aboard his warship, particularly "Charley the Cook."

With a straight face Waddell denied the charges. The Solicitor suggested that he send some of his men aboard to search the ship, but Waddell refused. He returned to the ship and pulled her to midstream "rather than submit to the humiliation of a search."

Again Waddell was asked if Charley was aboard the *Shenandoah,* and again he denied the charge. But it is apparent that Blanchard's agents were right; in his testimony in the Alabama Claims Hearing in Geneva in 1871, the United States consul pointed out that he returned to the office of the Crown Solicitor the day after Waddell had denied the charges, with proof that "Charley the cook and ten other men" had been arrested by the Melbourne "water police" as they left the *Shenandoah.*

"They were there all the time," Blanchard testified.[30]

Weeks passed. Under bombardment by Blanchard's affidavits and almost daily reports, the uneasy Australian government asked Waddell when he would leave. Waddell informed them that his ship needed more repairs.

In the legislature a member "produced a sensation" by

[30] Tribunal, p. 432.

describing the "war like makeup of the Shenandoah," evidence and details undoubtedly supplied by the intrepid Blanchard. The legislature was thrown into an uproar, with the presiding officer pounding his gavel and shouting for order while Confederate sympathizers demanded that the member be called out of order, which he was.

But the Australian press put the story on their front pages, thereby so disturbing the Governor that he informed the Crown Solicitor he thought Waddell was wearing out his welcome. The Solicitor took the hint, and sent his secretary to ask Waddell to name his departure date. The *Shenandoah's* skipper, who now felt the first coolness in the heretofore warm Australian cordiality, replied he would set sail as soon as he could load 300 tons of coal, "and swing my ship about . . ."

On the seventeenth, the day the *Shenandoah* was to sail, Blanchard triumphantly gathered the last of several affidavits, legal proof that Waddell was recruiting men for his raider. He rushed in a carriage to the office of the Australian Crown Solicitor, the man the Attorney General had told him to see, should he obtain this legal evidence.

As Blanchard indignantly described it in a letter to London, he met the Crown Solicitor coming out of his office.

"I am leaving for dinner," the Solicitor said.

"But I have urgent business. I have come as representative of the United States to lay before you the evidence that a large number of men are violating your neutrality laws."

Blanchard wrote: "The Solicitor said he had to go to his dinner, then passed on."

We can picture the consul in a white rage, followed by his cortege of uncomfortable seamen, as he got into his carriage and started off for the Attorney General's office.

28

There he received a courteous brush-off; the Attorney General sent him to another solicitor. By the time he had made the rounds, he was slowly strangled to death by red tape and the Australian love of extended dinner hours.

Australian officialdom was full of regrets, but Blanchard had his revenge a few years later when the United States filed her claim against England. Blanchard's run-around was described fully for the Tribunal, and he also included press accounts of how as many as eighty Australians had been recruited and had sailed with the Shenandoah.

"A simple train of reasoning will show the Tribunal of Arbitration that the least measure of diligence would have discovered the facts to the (Australian) authorities," he wrote.[31]

After leaving Melbourne, Waddell set a course first for the South Pacific, then the Arctic Ocean, where the Shenandoah roamed like a stalking wolf among the lumbering, helpless wooden whalers in the Sea of Okhotsk off Siberia. At that time whaling vessels remained at sea for long periods, and Waddell received little or no information about events in the world outside the Arctic.

In April, 1865, the Shenandoah cornered and sank four whalers in the harbor of Ascension, an island of the Caroline group in the Pacific.

On the morning of May 27 (Waddell's account gives the date as May 29), more than a month after Lee had surrendered, the Shenandoah captured and burned her first postwar victim in the Sea of Okhotsk off Siberia. She was the bark Abigail, out of San Francisco. The bark's captain, a fast-talking man, dressed in a fur coat and hat which gave

[31] Tribunal, pp. 445-447.

him the appearance of an indignant polar bear, begged Waddell to spare his ship and her cargoes of "notions" used in trading with the natives. After his pleas were refused he tried bribery. Waddell ignored him, and the *Abigail* became a crackling torch in the Arctic night.

One thing was spared, the ship's bundle of San Francisco newspapers. They carried stunning news—Lee had surrendered. Along with the front-line dispatches was news that part of Lee's army had joined General Johnston in North Carolina, and that President Jefferson Davis and his cabinet had moved the government to Danville. One dispatch carried an exhortation by Davis to the people of the Confederacy to carry on the struggle.

A council of war was held in the wardroom. Waddell gave his officers the facts and told them that as long as the government was resisting, he would continue to fulfill his mission. The officers agreed, and the *Shenandoah* moved deeper into the Sea of Okhotsk.

The raider kept capturing and burning ships so rapidly that soon there was no room left to stow the prisoners. By June 26 Waddell had to rig a chain of whaleboats to tow the officers and crews of the captured whalers.

On June 28, after a brisk chase, the *Shenandoah* captured twelve whalers. Nine were ordered burned. A spectator vividly described the sight of the fleet burning throughout the night among the ice floes:

> The red glare from the . . . burning vessels shone far and wide over the drifting ice of those savage seas; the crackling of the fire as it made its devouring way through each doomed ship, fell on the still air like upbraiding voices. The sea was filled with boats driving hither and thither with no hand to guide them, and with yards, sails and cordage, remnants of the

The *Shenandoah* towing prisoners from three burning whaling vessels in Bering Strait, June 25, 1865.

stupendous ruin there progressing. In the distance, but where the light fell strong and red upon them, bringing out into bold relief each spar and line, were the two ransomed vessels, the Noah's Arks that were to bear away the human life which in a few hours would be all that was left of the gallant whaling fleet . . . When, one by one, the burning hulks went hissing and gurgling down into the treacherous bosom of the ocean, the last act in the bloody drama of the American Civil War had been played.[32]

In one week Waddell had captured twenty-four of the fleet's fifty-eight whalers; twenty of New England's proudest whaling ships had gone to the bottom. And this feat was accomplished without the loss of a single life.

The files of the Atlantic Mutual Insurance Company reveal the terror which swept through northern shipping circles when news reached the West Coast from England that the *Shenandoah* was *on her way* to the Arctic. Actually, by that time, the fleet had been destroyed and scattered.

The insurance company's reports show that numerous terrified shipowners sought to insure their ships and cargoes against the "Confederate pirate," as Stanton described her. The insurance company accepted hundreds of applications— for a small premium, considering the risk involved—under an insurance clause containing the wording "lost or not lost." Under this clause, a vessel was insured as of a certain date even if it later developed that she had actually been destroyed or damaged prior to that time. It was understood, of course, that no word of the vessel's loss had reached the shipowner at the time the insurance became effective.

Atlantic Mutual satisfactorily negotiated all these transactions involving premiums of $350,000 by telegraph points

[32] *Cargoes*, No. 37, June, 1955. p. 1 (hereinafter cited as Cargoes).

32

through the North in just three days. During one day alone, the company received $118,978 in premiums—the largest sum written by Atlantic Mutual during a 24-hour period until the start of World War I. Aggregate losses paid by the company on vessels and cargoes destroyed by the *Shenandoah* amounted to $1,653,000.

The *Shenandoah* moved slowly among the towering icebergs, the whaleboats bobbing like corks in her wake. Muffled by a shawl and the upturned collar of a pea jacket, Waddell paced the quarterdeck, a desperate plan slowly forming in his mind. One newspaper had mentioned that the sole defense for the harbor of San Francisco was the Union warship *Saginaw*. As her former second officer, he knew her as well as he knew the back of his own hand. What was to prevent the *Shenandoah* from steaming into the harbor, sinking the *Saginaw*, and then turning her own heavy guns on the city. . . ?

When Waddell discussed the idea with his officers, they were cautious at first but gradually became enthusiastic. Throughout the long nights when the *Shenandoah*, groaning and creaking in every plank, made her way through the floes, the officers discussed how they would run their ship into San Francisco Bay under cover of darkness, ram the ironclad *Saginaw*, and board her. In the morning the city would wake to the crashing of their guns. After a prolonged bombardment, they would send a boat ashore to parlay for a sizable ransom.

While his officers made their grand, wild plans, Waddell limped about the deck, guiding his ship through fog and ice more by intuition than by instruments. Once they struck an iceberg. The *Shenandoah*'s bow bit deep. Below, men and officers off watch were flung from their bunks. There was pandemonium for a few minutes until Waddell, after re-gaining his feet, skillfully backed his ship off the ice and into open water. During the entire voyage through the ice-choked sea, he left the deck only to gulp down mugs of scalding coffee and some food. When they finally reached the open Pacific, he was so exhausted that he fell into his bunk and was asleep before an officer had cut off his sea boots.

Across the world in the quiet of his office at Trenholm and Fraser, Bulloch was sadly writing Waddell of the South's final surrender, the collapse of their government, and the arrest of President Davis. He ordered Waddell to spike the *Shenandoah*'s guns, pay off the crew, and cease raiding.

Earl Russell sent a vessel with this message, but it was not until August, 1865, that Waddell received word from an English bark of the South's surrender and Lincoln's assassination. When he read the news, the stricken Waddell ordered his ship's guns spiked, her stacks lowered, but left the salt-licked and wind-torn bit of Confederate bunting still flying.

The great raid into San Francisco's harbor was now but a bitter dream. The last armed resistance of the Confederate States of America had finally come to an end.

In his memoirs Waddell gives scant attention to the events which took place on his ship on the day he and his officers received the news of the South's surrender and in the last months of her voyage. There is reason to believe that the long voyage, the bitter days and nights in the Arctic, and the apprehension they all felt of meeting a powerful Federal cruiser affected discipline, and there is even testimony that the *Shenandoah* had become something of a hell ship in the last weeks of her cruise.

Doctor Lining and Midshipman Mason, in their day-to-day journals, now in the Virginia State Historical Society, mention drunkenness and occasional brawls.[33]

C. E. Hunt, in his short but valuable account of his experiences as an officer aboard the raider, published in London in 1866, charges that Waddell had turned into a vicious, unreasonable tyrant.[34]

Captain Waddell may have been humorless, single-minded, and tired at the time, but he was also proud and he refused to tarnish his honor or that of his ship by serving his own and the crew's interest at the cost of disobeying his country's orders, which were to return to Liverpool and surrender to British authorities.

To obey those orders Waddell had to sail 17,000 miles with a ship whose boilers were foul and salt-crusted and whose engines wheezed and groaned. He had to face the reality of typhoons and the hazard of meeting Federal cruisers which were out to capture or sink his ship.

His officers begged him to sail to Melbourne; none of them wanted to chance a trial in Washington on charges of piracy. Stanton wanted to hang them all.

Waddell had the choice of disobeying his orders and saving his own neck, or obeying and risking execution by a country already in the white heat of lynch rule because of the murder of its beloved President. He chose to return to

[33] "The Journal of Charles E. Lining," pub. in *A Calendar of Confederate Papers Prepared under the Direction of the Confederate Memorial Literary Society, Richmond, Virginia,* 1908. Lining was the surgeon aboard the *Shenandoah.* Also, the Journal of John T. Mason.
[34] Hunt, p. 269.

Liverpool. As he states very simply, it was "the honorable thing to do."

In my novel *Seek Out and Destroy*, which is based on the *Shenandoah's* cruise, I have a mutiny taking place on the fictional raider, the C.S.S. *Lee*. Although a mutiny did not break out on the *Shenandoah*, there are indications that one was simmering for days in the officers' wardroom.

In a letter written to a friend in Alabama in 1865, Waddell bitterly described the reaction of his officers upon learning of the South's surrender: "Among the officers I witnessed a terror which mortified me . . . their conduct was nothing less than mutiny . . . I had to tell one officer I would be captain or die in the deck . . ."[35]

On her return trip to England the *Shenandoah* had an angel on her foremast. Despite her salt-crusted boilers and her worn engines, she battled storms and dodged Federal cruisers. Waddell did not know it at the time, but he had narrowly escaped meeting the heavy warship *Iroquois*, Captain C. R. P. Rogers commanding. Rogers had received word of the *Shenandoah* when he sailed into Montevideo harbor. Without waiting to take on supplies, he stalked her across the Pacific, once missing the cruiser by a few weeks. But the lumbering Union warship was still no match for the sea-worn Confederate cruiser, which soon lost her in the vastness of the Arctic seas. Rear Admiral Pearson's Pacific Squadron was also criss-crossing the oceans for the *Shenandoah* after Secretary of the Navy Welles sent an order to him at Acapulco, Mexico, to find and destroy her at any cost. However, Pearson never sighted the raider.

Finally at 1:00 P.M., November 6, 1865, the weary *Shenan-*

[35] Hunt, p. 269. An extract from a letter written by Waddell in England to "a gentleman in Mobile, Alabama, Dec. 27, 1865."

The last page of the *Shenandoah*'s log. The cruiser surrendered to the British on November 7.

*doah,* now 172 days and 23,000 miles from the Aleutians, entered the Mersey River. She took a pilot aboard who promptly ran her aground on the bar. Waddell fumed as he limped about the quarterdeck, but there was nothing for him to do but wait for the tide to float her free.

The next morning, "still flying the Confederate Flag," as Dudley bitterly observed with his glasses, the *Shenandoah* moved up the Mersey and lowered the kedge at 1:00 P.M. The first British officer aboard H.M.S. *Donegal* who spoke her, gasped when he heard her name.

"My God," he called, "I was reading a few days ago of your being in the Arctic Ocean!"

Waddell surrendered the *Shenandoah* to Captain J. G. Paynter, commanding the *Donegal,* after he had dispatched a long letter to the Queen's Attorney detailing his cruise. He and his officers were not imprisoned but were asked to give their word as gentlemen not to leave the ship until their case had been decided. Young Hunt, who would make grave charges against his captain, was the only one to break his word.

The reappearance of the *Shenandoah* in England's waters startled Great Britain. She was already under heavy attack by the United States for having armed and equipped Bulloch's cruisers and tenders; the reappearance of the *Shenandoah* would only pour vinegar in the raw flesh of diplomatic relations. The London *Times* was quite blunt in denouncing the arrival of the cruiser as an "untoward and unwelcome event."

A study of the dispatches in the State Department—they flowed between Liverpool, London, and the United States at the time—reveals the tragedy, humor, and official confusion which followed in the wake of the Rebel raider. The

## THE DISPUTED ACCOUNT.

*Britannia.* "CLAIM FOR DAMAGES AGAINST *ME?* NONSENSE, COLUMBIA: DON'T BE MEAN OVER MONEY MATTERS."

A cartoon in London's *Punch* when the United States was demanding that England pay damages for the ships sunk by the *Alabama* and *Shenandoah*.

39

moment the lookout in Liverpool's watchtower spread the word along the cobbled streets that the *Shenandoah* had entered the Mersey, U.S. Consul Thomas H. Dudley and Vice-Consul H. Wilding touched off the diplomatic wars. Two hours after the *Shenandoah* had let out her anchor chain, Wilding telegraphed a detailed picture of her arrival to Adams at the American Legation in London. Apparently Dudley's spy system was still operating smoothly. In his dispatch, Wilding pointed out they had information that "aboard the Shenandoah are a number of chronometers taken from vessels destroyed."

At 3:00 P.M. Adams was calling on the Earl of Clarendon at the Foreign Office in London. When he told Clarendon the news, the nobleman, as Adams wrote Washington, "was utterly incredulous." He admitted the Admiralty had given him the same news shortly before Adams had arrived and he had found it hard to believe.

After his brief visit, Adams sent the Earl a formal note containing details of the Confederate cruiser's arrival. He called for the British government "to secure the party aboard this corsair," and as for Waddell, the officers, and the crew, he added: "I venture to hope that Her Majesty's government will be induced voluntarily to adopt that action which may most satisfy my countrymen."

A few days later he wrote a complete report to Secretary of State Seward in Washington. He outlined the action he had taken, explaining that he believed he had only two "courses" to follow—take over custody of the *Shenandoah* and let Great Britain take the responsibility of meting out justice to Waddell and his men.

Adams ended his report on this bitter note: "If we demand that the men be turned over to us as war prisoners they will say hostilities are ended. If we charge them as pirates they will demand proof . . . and should a trial be held it will probably turn out a farce, as all preceding appeals to the judicial tribunals have been during this struggle. In either case the full responsibility must rest with this country . . ."

In the next few days there was an exchange of stiff and formal notes between Adams and the British Foreign Office. Finally, the Earl of Clarendon announced that as far as the British government was concerned, Captain Waddell and his officers were not guilty of any charges and were free. However, Clarendon ordered Captain Paynter to interrogate the crew members and determine if any were British subjects who had violated their country's Foreign Enlistment Act.[36]

The *Shenandoah* was lashed to the British gunboat *Goshawk* and placed under the broadsides of the *Donegal's* guns while Captain Paynter questioned the crew in the wardroom. Consul Dudley was later shocked to hear how the questioning had been conducted. The British and Scottish seamen, coached by their American shipmates, rattled off the names of towns and cities in the Confederate states from which they allegedly came, with broad Scottish burrs and cockney accents. Captain Paynter listened with grave face and let them all go.

Waddell had landed with the ship's treasury, variously estimated from "$820.28 in mixed gold and silver" to £20,000, which he immediately deposited with Lloyds of London. This, in addition to the money which remained in Bulloch's "Public Fund," was given to the officers for transportation

[36] Bulloch, *Secret Service*, Vol. II, p. 140.

and to the crew members to satisfy the bonuses Waddell
had promised in the Arctic. After his men had been paid
off, Waddell suffered a ruptured blood vessell and remained
at the Waterloo Hotel in Liverpool for several months,
recuperating. Some of his officers, including Surgeon Lining
and Midshipman Mason, went to Buenos Aires to join a
colony of expatriated Confederates.

After Waddell and his men left the ship, the *Shenandoah*
remained in the Mersey. Adams was demanding that she be
turned over to the United States, and the British Foreign
Office was trying to make up its mind what to do with this
sea-scarred vessel which now was a diplomatic nuisance.

While Adams was pressing the Earl of Clarendon for a
decision, Vice-Consul Wilding in Liverpool just could not
keep away from the *Shenandoah*. As he reported to Dudley,
he paid a visit to the ship in November and asked the Collector of Port, who had charge of the cruiser, what he intended to do with her.

"Are you here in an official capacity or privately?" the
Collector asked cautiously.

"Well, I have no instructions, so I guess I'm here privately," Wilding replied.

"Well, then I can tell you," the Collector said. "I don't
know what to do. I haven't received any instructions."

Wilding returned to his Liverpool office and told Dudley.
Then he wrote a report of the visit for Seward, adding:
"Although the arrival of the Shenandoah has caused a great
deal of talk here, most people would approve of Captain
Waddell being dealt with and delivered up as a pirate."

Great Britain at last turned the ship over to the United
States, no doubt with a great sigh of relief. Adams telegraphed Dudley the news, and told him to make immediate

arrangements to have her taken to New York. Dudley, in turn, telegraphed Rear Admiral Goldsborough, requesting enough officers and men to sail the cruiser across the Atlantic.

An aide replied that the message had been delivered to the Admiral, who was in the Mediterranean area, and that Goldsborough had instructed him to refuse Dudley's request. He pointed out: "The Admiral is not satisfied the government at home relished acceptance of the Shenandoah and for this and other reasons he has declined to detail officers and men to sail the ship to the United States."

Dudley sent this reply on to Adams, who apparently resented the somewhat arrogant refusal, because he in turn got in touch with Goldsborough. The Admiral was more diplomatic in his reply to the United States Minister to the Court of St. James than he had been to Dudley. As Adams reported to Seward, Goldsborough explained that he was short-staffed and could not carry out the assignment "unless I expressly requested him to do so."

After reporting to Seward, Adams instructed Dudley to make what arrangements he could to get the *Shenandoah* to the States. Dudley replied, in a few days, that he had found Captain Thomas F. Freeman, whom he proudly described as "an American citizen and a fine seaman." Freeman, he said, was willing to sail the *Shenandoah* to New York. Adams approved Dudley's suggestion, and Freeman, a veteran ship's captain for Williams and Guion, a large New York exporting company, took over the *Shenandoah.*

On the morning tide of November 21, 1865, Freeman and fifty-five officers and men sailed for the United States. On December 6, the *Shenandoah,* "short of coal and loss of sails," returned to Liverpool.

Judging from his report to Adams, which the Minister sent on to the State Department in Washington, Freeman appears to have suffered a terrifying ordeal in the wintry ocean. No sooner had they reached the open sea, he said, than the *Shenandoah*'s screw, which had given Waddell trouble in the early days of his cruise, began vibrating so badly it shook the ship from forefoot to stern.

Freeman had the screw lifted into its well and the sails set. Just as this was done, a raging storm fell on the ship with a wild fury. The fore-topsail was split to the deck, and the spars came crashing down. In two days the sails were tattered rags. The damaged screw was then lowered, and for days the *Shenandoah* rode out the storm. Mountainous waves tossed her about like a chip in a millrace. White water covered her decks from bow to stern. There were times when she plunged so deep Freeman thought she could never rise again. But the gallant ship did, groaning and crying out in every plank as she lifted her bow from beneath the tons of water which tried to sink her. Then the galley fires went out, and the crew was forced to eat hardtack and drink cold water.

After the fourth day, the skies cleared temporarily and the ship's carpenter cleared the debris. But then the thunderheads thickened and another winter storm fell on the crippled ship. Freeman had now had enough. As he wrote, it would have been suicidal to keep on. He turned back to England. The *Shenandoah* was still the last unchained Rebel.

In Liverpool Freeman had more trouble. His weary crew refused to work, and as he reported to Dudley, "Rather than put them in irons, I sent them ashore."

At Dudley's request, Freeman closely inspected the *Shen-*

*andoah;* he pronounced her seaworthy, but suggested she be given "a new suit of sails," 130 tons of coal, a new crew, and ballast, before sending her out to sea again.

The American Legation, which had fought so hard to obtain custody of the cruiser, now found that she had become one of the largest white elephants of the postwar period. When Dudley and Adams tried to rehire Captain Freeman, he declined, pointing out that his company refused to allow him to take another risk.

Dudley tried to hire another captain and crew, but the Liverpool seamen refused to sign on. There seemed to be an aura of death and violence about the *Shenandoah*. She lay at her pier, proud in her loneliness, still sleek and still dangerous despite the ragged sails that dropped from her spars and the dull copper that showed where the ice floes of the Arctic had rubbed away her paint.

Although Waddell does not say so, the *Shenandoah* was too near his heart and his dreams for him not to have gone to the dock to visit her. The Waterloo Hotel, where he was convalescing, was only a short carriage ride from the waterfront. After all, there was nothing left for him to do but wait —Stanton, President Johnson, and Congress were still calling him the "Anglo-Rebel Pirate Captain." The New England whaling companies, the private shipowners, and the insurance companies who had suffered so much at his hands were still demanding that he be refused amnesty. Like Captain Tom Hines, the Confederate Agent who walked to the Windsor ferry on the Canadian side to look across the water at his homeland, Captain Waddell—we can believe—stood at the Liverpool dock many a chilly twilight during that long winter of discontent to gaze sadly at the deserted ship which was so much a part of him.

45

Adams realized that the *Shenandoah* was now a millstone. He sent Seward a few notes, including Captain Freeman's report on his trip, and reminded Seward the *Shenandoah* was "still anchored in the Mersey."

Then on January 26, 1866, the cruiser again exploded into the headlines of American and English newspapers. Congress, prodded no doubt by the shipowners and the insurance companies, passed a resolution formally demanding that President Johnson give a full accounting of "what order if any, he has taken in relation to the surrender of the Anglo-Rebel Pirate crew."

Johnson turned the request over to the State Department, and Acting Secretary of State W. Hunter compiled a report of all the letters sent to the department by Adams, Dudley, and Wilding. This report was submitted to Congress by President Johnson. There were some subsequent wild speeches by congressmen who demanded Waddell's neck, but on the whole Congress accepted Johnson's explanation that everything had been done that could have been done. From demanding that Waddell be put on trial as a pirate, Congress turned to a more popular subject: making England pay for the damages sustained by American shipowners. It was estimated that more than 30,000 claimants were clamoring for cash settlements.

The years dragged on, with the *Shenandoah* periodically appearing in the news.

In 1871 the Treaty of Washington was signed between the United States and England, and the Alabama Claims Commission was founded. It was agreed that there were to be five members selected by the United States, England, Italy, the President of the Swiss Confederation, and the Emperor of Brazil. The United States selected Charles Fran-

cis Adams, who was president of the court; England, Sir
Alexander James Edmund Cockburn, Lord Justice of Eng-
land; Italy, Count Frederick Sclopis, Minister of State; the
Swiss Confederation, M. James Stampfli, and Brazil, Marcos
Antonio D'Aracijo, a member of His Majesty's Privy Council.

The hearings were held in Geneva and Washington; they
finally resulted in a claim of $15,000,000 being paid by
England. Then the award itself became controversial. In
May, 1873, New York State rushed through a law that after
the insurance companies were "duly paid expenses and
liabilities," the rest of the money should be shared by
premium holders, some of whom had been forced into bank-
ruptcy when their ships and cargoes had been burned by the
*Shenandoah.*

By 1875, the *Shenandoah* was a memory. A decade had
passed since Lee's surrender. Thaddeus Stevens was dead,
and his congressional clique was fast dying off. Confederate
military leaders, now congressmen or senators, were back in
Washington dining with men against whom they had fought
from Bull Run to the Wilderness. There were still hate and
bitterness in the land, but time was healing the wounds.

Waddell finally returned to the United States in 1875. In
the fall of that year he was appointed captain of the liner
*San Francisco,* fresh from the ways, pride of the Pacific Mail
Line. The ship had been built by the company to sail the
route from New York to Melbourne.

Waddell's first stop was at Melbourne. Ten years had
passed since he had sailed the proud *Shenandoah* into that
port, but the Australians showed they had not forgotten him.
It was probably one of the most moving moments in Waddell's life when he gazed down on the welcoming crowd
cheering his name. There might be no sound of trumpets

for him in his native land, but here he was regarded as a seaman who could take his place among Elizabeth's captains.

Finally the last party had been held in his honor. The last piece of cargo was hoisted aboard, the last passenger waved good-by. The gleaming new 4,000-ton liner set sail on her maiden voyage to the United States. But bad luck was trailing in Waddell's wake. Fourteen miles off the coast of Mexico, under clear and sparkling skies, with a calm sea, the *San Francisco* went aground on a reef unmarked on any of the navigation charts. Waddell brought the liner to within three miles of the coast before she sank. No lives were lost, and in the best tradition of the sea he was the last to leave her. Ironically, the reef had been discovered in 1863, but in the confusion of war the Navy Department had never charted it. It is irony to top irony that the *Shenandoah*, like the *San Francisco*, would also tear her heart out on an unmarked reef.

The Pacific Mail Company did not blame Waddell, and he remained with them as a captain for several years before he finally retired to the quiet of Annapolis. In the eighties, the Governor of Maryland appointed him to take charge of the war that state was waging against the Chesapeake Bay oyster pirates. After several raids, Waddell's small force wiped out the pirates.

His hair now white, his step slower, Waddell continued to make his home in Annapolis, where once he had been a midshipman. He died here March 15, 1886.

Before he died Waddell wrote his memoirs, purely for his family's history. The year after his death his widow loaned the manuscript to General Marcus J. Wright, C.S.A. At that time General Wright was employed by the government as an agent for the collection of Confederate records, preparatory to the publication by the government of the *Official Records of the Union and Confederate Navies and Armies.* A portion of Waddell's manuscript in its edited form was used in the *Official Records.*

Today Waddell's memoirs are in the Archives of Naval Records, National Archives. The copy typed from his handwritten manuscript was edited by someone who not only corrected certain of his minor geographical mistakes but also removed some of the flavor of his dramatic story. Unseamanlike phrases in the manuscript are evidence that such was probably the case. I don't believe Waddell would ever have used such an expression as "ten knots an hour," for example, but a landlubber typist might unconsciously have altered the phrasing while copying the manuscript.

The log of the *Shenandoah* is in the Chicago Historical Society. I have found only a few unimportant Waddell letters in the Hotze and Mason Papers in the Library of Congress and in the National Archives. His one real memorial is this memoir now in the National Archives.

Waddell's friend and superior officer, James Dunwoody Bulloch, is another important figure in the hazy history of the Confederate cruisers who refused to leave any documents for historians except the two volumes of his memoirs. Like Mason and Slidell, he never returned to his native land. He elected to stay in Liverpool, where he became a prominent member of the city's social and shipping circles. Bulloch died on January 7, 1901.

For the last five years I have searched without success for clues that might lead me to Bulloch's cache of official orders, letters, and other papers relating to his wartime activity as Confederate Naval Agent in Europe. The Confederate Research Club of England, particularly its energetic secretary-treasurer, Patrick Courtney, has been most diligent in this field, even searching out Bulloch's kin in western Australia, but to no avail. I believe that either Bulloch or some member of his family destroyed his correspondence.[37]

And what of the *Shenandoah,* that "long and rakish ship" whose forefoot cut the waves of every ocean from the North Atlantic to the icy waters of the Okhotsk Sea?

After the almost fatal voyage to New York in the winter of 1866, and the failure of the American Legation to hire another captain and crew to take her back to the States, Adams decided to expedite the problem by putting her on the auction block. She was finally sold to the Sultan of Zanzibar—"his sable Majesty," as Bulloch called him—for $108,632.18. The Sultan said he intended to outfit the cruiser as a luxury yacht, but apparently his builders told him that the cost would be exorbitant. So he renamed her the *Majidi* and assigned her as a freighter to transport ivory, gum, and coal.

She was soon only a ghost of her own legend. In 1872 a hurricane wrecked the Sultan's entire fleet as it lay anchored at Zanzibar. The *Shenandoah* or *Majidi* was flung up on the beach and left to rot. A few months later, a British salvage company pulled her off the beach, patched her up so that she was watertight, and towed her to Bombay for repairs.

In his *Gallant Rebel,* Stanley F. Horn picks up the *Shenandoah* in July, 1872, after she had left the Bombay shipyards. She had put to sea with a German captain and native crew. Some weeks later a British warship, the *Briton,* picked

[37] Correspondence between the author and Patrick Courtney, secretary-treasurer of the Confederate Research Club of England, 1955-58.

up several survivors in the Mozambique Channel. They told a wild story of how the *Shenandoah* had been scuttled. The captain of the *Briton,* without supplying evidence, said he believed the German captain had scuttled the *Shenandoah* "because he wanted the Sultan to buy a ship from Hamburg."

Horn's version of the death of the *Shenandoah* is at variance with Bulloch's memoirs. Bulloch states that in 1879 the raider tore out her bottom on an unchartered reef in the Indian Ocean and sank. He points out that the wreck supplied the "leader" for *London Daily Telegraph,* which recounted the *Shenandoah's* great exploits.[38]

How she died was not important; the *Shenandoah* was home again.

[38] Bulloch, *Secret Service,* Vol. II, p. 187.

Lieutenant Commanding James I. Waddell, C.S.N.

52

# *The Memoirs of James I. Waddell*

# CHAPTER ONE

I was born in Pittsboro, Chatham County, North Carolina, —a hamlet far removed from salt water,—and when a little fellow, my paternal Grandmother adopted me, and for a few years thereafter I was taught the rudiments of education in a school conducted by a very estimable lady, who did not believe in moral suasion.

I must have been an incorrigible youngster. All the deviltry committed in and out of that hamlet the mothers of my playmates laid at my door and would exclaim, "I'll bet it was James Iredell," and that estimable school mistress believed it too.[1]

Mr. Alfred Moore, my maternal Grandfather, named me for that distinguished statesman and jurist. It became necessary, owing to the delicate health of my guardian, to remove me to my Grandfather's residence in Orange County, North Carolina, and at the age of 13 years, I was sent to Bingham's School in Hillsboro, N. C.

It is singular that the deviltry which my playmates'

[1] Waddell's full name was James Iredell Waddell.

mothers invariably ascribed to me went on as of old, and that I lost all desire for that amusement after leaving Chatham County. Perhaps the breezes of a loftier region sweeping over the red hills of old Orange purified my heart. It is, however, no less affectionately disposed towards my boyhood association, and I very often dwell in thought with loving reverence for those I knew so well, long years ago, and who have left me here, no longer the boy.

When Mr. Badger was Secretary of the Navy[2] he conferred on me an acting midshipman's appointment, and at the same time I received an order to report to Commodore William B. Shubrick for duty on board the ship of the line Pennsylvania, the only three-decker in the Naval service and pierced for one hundred and twenty guns.

The Pennsylvania was at her moorings in the Elizabeth River, off the Naval Hospital, Norfolk, Va. I had never seen a boat, I had no conception of a ship-of-war, or other floating armament. I was conscious of my ignorance, and I maintained a silence that was wonderful for one so young.

I reported for duty, and I shall never forget the intelligent advice given to me by Commodore Shubrick.

He said, "Young gentleman you must remember that you are now a servant of the people. They are taxed for your support, and you should at all times be respectful to the people. They can dismantle the Navy whenever they choose to exercise the power."

I have oftentimes reflected and regretted how fast and indifferent naval men have grown to the people and that power. I was astonished at what I saw in and about the Norfolk Navy yard. A new and very interesting world was

[2] George E. Badger, Secretary of the Navy, 1841, under President Harrison.

open to me. I asked no questions. What I saw did not seem unfamiliar, but it was the magnitude and variety of work that astonished me, the smoothness with which everything moved, the busy people ever on the go, and the salutations observed between superiors and subordinates.

I was directed to Tarrant and London, merchant tailors, where I would purchase the uniforms, and in a few days I was equipped and saw for the first time the Pennsylvania. Can you wonder at my surprise? It seemed an endless undertaking from the water up the companion ladder to the spar deck.

Once landed, I saw that she was hollow, and I felt I had never seen so many people together, and for what purpose?

The officer to whom I had a letter of introduction, Lieutenant Muse, was on deck, and I presented the letter. He took me in charge, sent me to report to the Commanding Officer, Lieutenant Adams, and I was installed in duties of which I had not the most remote idea. The night of the day I had reported for duty, I kept the mid watch from 12 to 4 A.M., and I kept a sharp lookout, feeling that there must be something in it, and in fulfillment of my duty I stopped walking the deck to take a good look, when the officer of the watch called out, "Mr. Waddell (I had never before heard my name accented), walk the deck, Sir."

I had been reared in tenderness, and so untutored to harsh discipline that the gruff manner and stern tone of Lieutenant Kieth so greatly shocked me I doubted his gentility.

It was in December, 1841, that I reached Norfolk, and entered upon my naval career. There were a number of acting midshipmen of all sizes, ages and dispositions,—there were those who had grown to manhood, and there were others who were boys in every sense of the word. I belonged to the latter class, of an independent, restless nature.

The material of which boys are made is always tested in that profession, by a more experienced and expert manhood, and it fell to my lot to be severely injured in May, 1842, which caused me to lose eleven months of professional service.[3] I was little advanced beyond the period of my debut when I returned to duty. So soon as I had gathered strength to move about, and a return of health seemed assured, I asked for orders, and the next mail brought me an order to join the sloop of war Vandalia, one of the Gulf Squadron.

There were no steam vessels in the Navy at that time. I served in that vessel for three years in the Gulf of Mexico and Windward Islands, under two commanders, McCluny and Chauncey. During that cruise the vessel was afflicted on three occasions with yellow fever, and we lost valuable officers and more than half her crew. I was at the bedside of Hooe when he died, and I love his memory. He was the Executive Officer of the Vandalia. I then served in the steamer Colonel Hasmy, which vessel was dispatched for the Brazos River, for General Taylor's use. Her boilers were in such bad condition she never got beyond New Orleans.

I was then ordered to the famous brig-of-war Somers, Duncan N. Ingraham, Commander, and I proceeded to join her at Pensacola, and I entered on my old occupation of cruising in the Gulf of Mexico.

When it became certain that General Taylor would engage the Mexican Army, Commodore Conner, a very plain

[3] Waddell does not mention it, but the reason for the loss of his "professional service" was a wound he received in a duel with a classmate. The wound he suffered made him limp for the rest of his life.

old gentleman, no fuss and feathers about him, directed his fleet to proceed with despatch from Vera Cruz to Point Isabel, the base of General Taylor's supplies.

The Somers was first to arrive there, and Commander Ingraham detailed from his command a force, and held it in readiness to land in aid of protecting military stores, and for other purposes.

Lieutenant Clairbourne, the Executive Officer, informed the midshipmen, three in number, to draw lots which two should accompany the landing force. I drew a blank.

The vessel was near enough for the people on board to hear the roar of artillery and rattle of musketry, our hearts were with our countrymen. After the defeat of the enemy, Commodore Conner returned his fleet to Vera Cruz.

From the Somers I was ordered to report to Commander Franklin Buchanan, Superintendent of the Naval school, Annapolis, Md. I landed at Pensacola from the store ship Relief, and proceeded overland, reaching Annapolis in January, 1841. The class of 1841 originally numbered two hundred and fifty. In consequence of the small accommodation at the Naval school, and the existence of war, the Secretary of the Navy decided to divide the class into three batches.

The midshipmen had seen sea service and were young seamen. I candidly think there never was a class of more promising young naval sea officers, and young men possessing talent enough to grace any profession which inclination might induce them to embrace.

I passed the examination with the second batch of midshipmen,—I say passed, because I prefer it to being considered a graduate. The all important, useful and necessary branches of my profession, I learned at sea, on ship board, while a boy.

The training which Naval Cadets receive, is admirable, and the education makes them useful citizens, and strengthens the defense of the country. It is claimed they are unfitted for civil occupation after six years of naval life. In my experience, they are better adapted to civil occupation for that naval training, than they are for naval life, because ships and the management of ships, they do not understand, and cannot with that limited experience, and the seamanship they know is not so impressed on their brain that they cannot drop it without an effort.

I may be in error when I assert that practical seamanship cannot be learned from books, nor can it be learned as lastingly after manhood, as it can be during boyhood. I therefore think the selections made from the offspring of forty millions of people would make a better return to the Government if the successful aspirants after examination at the Naval Academy were immediately sent to sea for the term of five years, because ships and the management of ships would be learned practically during boyhood, and in those five years the objectionable ones would be gotten rid of. And after five years afloat, have them examined on board their respective vessels, in seamanship.

Those whose moral tone, professional aptitude and knowledge of seamanship fitted them for the naval service, should be recommended for a full course of study at the Naval Academy, by the respective shipboard examiners.

Those who graduated in all the useful branches, including seamanship, should be assigned rank in the naval service, not below that of Master, and make it a reward after nine years of meritorious service. I think such a system would be

58

productive of a vast good to the country. And those Naval Cadets who failed to graduate, being young seamen, could enter the merchant service, elevate the standard of that service, because of a better and more exalted training, and of an intelligence, superior.

It is impossible for a graduate (at this writing) of the Naval Academy to be a practical seaman, and as I am a tax paying citizen of the U.S., and a lover of the sea and ships, I should be gratified to feel that the Naval Graduate was more practical and knew less of non-essentials to the profession, for all of which the Congress of the U.S. is to blame.

Professional men, from causes, are very often debarred the opportunity to acquire generous education, yet, subsequent events develop in them an aptitude for professional distinction, which register their names high in their country's history. And it is peculiarly applicable to the American.

The test of merit is success, I know it is a hard rule, but it is nevertheless just. Before taking leave of the Naval Academy and looking back through the years since I left it, I think to Commander Franklin Buchanan is due the credit for its establishment, more than to any other person,—it has become what he never intended it to be. Admiral Buchanan was a chivalrous gentleman, he had no superior, professional or otherwise.

After receiving the certificate of graduation, I was ordered home, and after a short leave, I was ordered to the National Observatory, and was assigned duty on the wind and current charts. My sojourn there was of short duration.

I preferred duty at the Naval Academy, and I was ordered to the Executive Department. From the Naval Academy I was ordered to the frigate Independence, the flag ship of the Mediterranean Squadron, Commodore Morgan, Commander-in-Chief.

After a year's service in that vessel, I was ordered to the store ship Relief, Benjamin J. Totten, Lieutenant Commanding, and returned to the U.S. My health failed on that homeward trip, and a surgeon's certificate placed me on sick leave.

In a few months I was all right again, and I received orders to the Naval Academy in the Executive Department, and I made the summer cruises with the cadet midshipmen. I was ordered from the Naval Academy to the sloop of war Germantown, and that vessel was absent forty-three months on the Brazil station.

I began that cruise a Passed Midshipman, and returned in her to the U.S. the second Lieutenant. I was continued navigator by her Commander. I believe it to be the first instance where the second Lieutenant of an American man-of-war was required to do navigator's duty. At the present date of the Naval service, the second lieutenants of vessels are the navigators.

I was detached from the Germantown and given three months' leave of absence. I was at home just seven weeks when I was ordered to the store ship Release, and the vessel went to Aspinwall[4] with stores for the Pacific Squadron.

While at Aspinwall, I became acquainted with Engineer Fulton, the builder of the Panama railroad. He told me ten thousand men had been buried along the line of that road. That the climate had defeated the Negroes imported from the Islands to do the work of building the railroad, and that white men had come from all parts of the world for the same employment and had succeeded.

[4] Aspinwall (Colón), Panama.

Before leaving Aspinwall I was attacked by the fever. Two days thereafter the Release went to sea, and from day to day, someone was stricken, until the vessel's compliment [*sic*] of men was reduced to one seaman and one boy. I was convalescent and returned to duty.

The seaman and myself alternately took the wheel. Our supply of quinine was exhausted. Brazier appreciated the danger to which his command was exposed, prudently close-reefed the topsails. We were favored by fair and stiff winds, —a gale might perhaps have been fatal,—some of the people were delirious, none able to lend a hand. We fell in with a vessel and secured a small quantity of quinine.

Brazier was stricken with the fever and I was the only officer on duty to care for the vessel. Before reaching the port of Mantanzas, the Captain directed me to go for that port. I had never been there, I had a chart of the harbor.

The vessel had entered the harbor when a pilot came alongside. He discovered our condition and left us. The captain had become delirious from fever, and came on deck in his shirt tail, I feared he would go overboard, he however looked astern and then returned to his cabin.

There was nothing left me but to undertake the pilotage, and I succeeded in taking the vessel safely to the anchorage. We remained in port five days. The men were recovering, and enough had returned to duty to render the vessel safe at sea.

The Captain's orders were, on his return from Aspinwall to proceed to the Boston Navy Yard. After being at sea several days, our condition did not seem so hopeful as when we left port. The Captain and most of the officers had not sufficiently recovered. We had at that date, by aid of good winds and the Gulf Stream, gone rapidly Northward, and the Captain addressed a letter to the officers, asking an exchange of sentiment, as to the propriety of his taking the vessel to New York instead of Boston, and would the circumstances existing on board, justify him in going to New York?

I felt uncomfortable, when I was told I was the only officer who advised the captain to obey his orders. The result was the Release was taken to Boston, laid up and everybody detached from her.

I returned home. In a very short time I was ordered to the receiving-vessel at Baltimore, Commander Robert F. Pinkney, Commanding, and entered on my duties as the Executive Officer. In a few months I was again ordered to the Naval Academy in the Executive Department, and my old association was renewed under Commander Thomas T. Craven,[5] Commandant of Midshipmen, for whom I have an affectionate remembrance, and to whom I am very indebted for the better part of the knowledge I possess, of my profession.

All the officers, with the exception of now Rear-Admiral Craven, are dead, with whom I was associated in that Department, and they were as companionable gentlemen as the sunlight ever shone upon.

I feel I have been here a long time, for I can now count on my fingers those heroic souls who battled the watch and the weather with me,—nearly all have gone, and I too soon must follow.

---

[5] Ironically, Commodore Craven, commanding the U.S.S. *Niagara*, would be court-martialed for refusing to fight the C.S.S. *Stonewall*, the one ram the Confederacy would get to sea, off the coast of Spain in February, 1865. He was ordered suspended for two years, but the case was retried. Finally he was acquitted.

# CHAPTER TWO

The steamer Saginaw was under construction at Mare Island, California, Commodore Cunningham was in command of the station. I was ordered in July, 1859, to report to Commodore Cunningham for duty on the Saginaw. In obedience to the order I took passage in a Pacific mail steamship via Panama.

Commander James Findlay Schenck was assigned the Saginaw. Bayse N. Westcott was Executive Officer. I was second Lieutenant, Marshall Campbell was third Lieutenant. Charles McDougal was Sailing Master, and Samuel F. Cours passed Assistant Surgeon. Medical Director Cours is alive, the others are dead I believe.

When I arrived at Mare Island you may imagine my disgust at being separated from my family, when the evidence of the work to be done on the steamer would take all of six months. We were quartered on board of the Independence, the same old ship I had been in in the Mediterranean several years before, and there we remained until the spring of 1860, before we sailed for the China station.

The Saginaw was a political vessel. The Secretary of the Navy ordered her to be built at the instigation of Dr. Gwin, the Duke of Sonora. It was very well known that California timber was unfit for ship building, the cost double what she would have cost if she had been built in the East. The laurel of California is fit only for furniture. The Saginaw was built of laurel, and she was never considered seaworthy.

However, we succeeded in making all the Islands on route to Hong Kong, and finally we arrived at Hong Kong. We escaped the violence of a typhoon in crossing the China Sea, but damage enough was done to require repairs. The squadron was commanded by Commodore C. K. Stribling, and the squadron moved northward to the Gulf of Pecheli,[6] where the English and French forces were assembling to attack the Chinese fortifications.

After our arrival in the Gulf, Minister Ward came on board and the Saginaw was taken into the river Piho[7] which empties into the Gulf of Pecheli. When the allies were ready for the attack, in front and in the rear, it was only a matter of a few hours fighting before the fortifications all fell into their hands. I was an eye witness to the advance of an English Naval brigade, and I saw an officer who was gallantly leading it, through a shower of iron and leaden hail, fall. He was on his feet as quickly as he was down, and kept the lead.

Ten years after this circumstance I have just narrated, a state dinner was given, in the city of Annapolis, by his Excellency Governor Wm. Bowie to the Captain and officers of H.B.M. steamer Monarch, the same which brought to this country the remains of Mr. George Peabody. Captain Sir John Commerell commanded the Monarch.

At that dinner Commerell sat on Mrs. Bowie's left, and the Governor assigned me to Commerell's left. We soon engaged in professional talk, and I stated what I had witnessed on the banks of the Piho. Captain Commerell re-

[6] Gulf of Chihili or Pechili, now Gulf of Po Hai, the northwest arm of the Yellow Sea.
[7] River Pai-ho.

marked, "I was that officer who fell, I was hit by a spent ball."

The Saginaw was ordered to Hong Kong, and there we began to hear something about political affairs in the United States. Each mail succeeded in bringing intensified news and rumors of civil war. The sloop of war John Adams, Commander John M. Berrien, had seen her service, and was getting ready to return to the United States.

I was detached from the Saginaw, and ordered to the John Adams. I was pleased to receive the order, I had determined if the North made war on the South to go South and assist those people. I hoped there would be peace between the sections, war would intensify hatred, without even a hope of ever restoring good fellowship, it mattered not which were victorious. I still hoped for a better feeling to prevail.[8]

In this condition of political affairs at home, the John Adams sailed en route for New York. The passage was good enough, but it was unnecessarily prolonged. I think we reached the Island of St. Helena in the latter part of November, 1861, and it was then we received our first intelligence of actual war—the result of the Battle of Bull Run.

My correspondence was sad indeed. So soon as I had finished reading my letter which met me at St. Helena, I wrote my resignation and sent it through Commander Berrien, to the Secretary of the Navy. It could not take effect until the vessel's return had been reported to the Navy Department.

[8] Apparently the naval officers then in the United States service were more coolheaded than the army officers, who were resigning in large numbers. Bulloch, like Waddell, at this time was waiting to make his choice, hoping that peace would be maintained.

*COPY*

U. S. Ship John Adams,<br>
St. Helena, 20 November, 1861.

To the Hon.
The Secretary of the Navy:
Sir:

The people of the State of North Carolina having withdrawn their allegiance to the Government, and the State from the Confederacy of the United States; and owing to these circumstances, and for reasons to be hereafter mentioned, I return to his Excellency the President of the United States, the commission which appointed me a Lieutenant in the Navy, with other public documents, asking acceptance thereof.

In thus separating myself from associations which I have cherished for twenty years, I wish it to be understood that no doctrine of the right of secession, no wish for disunion of the States impel me, but simply because, my home is the home of my people in the South, and I cannot bear arms against it or them.

I am, Sir, respectfully,<br>
James I. Waddell.

Hon. Gideon Welles.


As a naval man, human character is a study, or should be a study, and first impressions are with me generally correct and very lasting. Opinions never alter my convictions, as I understand, so have I acted, and when I take a retrospect, I have no feeling for regret. Opinion is a cheap commodity, people are fond of expressing opinions, they are very harmful with the weak, and the unfortunate are the only sufferers by such offensive people.

In January, 1862, the John Adams arrived at the New York Navy Yard; the war excitement was intense, and the brutal languages employed by individuals towards Southern people fell upon my ear at every turn. I called on the Paymaster to draw the money due me, he answered he had received instructions to transfer settlement to the Navy Department. I was visited by an old and valued friend, Lieutenant Watson Smith, who had been a classmate and roommate at the Naval School; he came in the name of Commander David D. Porter to offer to me the command of the left wing of the bomb fleet, then in a state of preparation for New Orleans; I declined the honor. My old friend Watson Smith said, "I shall not respect friendship on the field." I was surprised, for never had he talked to me in that way before, should we ever confront each other on the field, I certainly would feel more inclined to engage a stranger than a classmate, a roommate and a messmate; I was friendly to Watson Smith, and I was pained to say in reply, "I shall be pleased to meet you, since you shall not respect friendship on the field." We never met afterwards, he died during the war.

I carefully considered my surroundings and situation. Have you read Mr. Isaacs? Mr. Isaacs said to Mr. Griggs, "I suppose you have no conscience?" Mr. Griggs: "Political conscience? No, certainly not. Out of my own country, which is the only one where that sort of thing commands a high salary, *no* I have no conscience." Just so with me. I addressed the following letter.

*COPY*

Annapolis, Maryland,
January 24, 1862.

His Excellency
Abraham Lincoln,
President of the United States:
Sir:

I deem it my duty to the Government which I have served from my boyhood, to state to your Excellency candidly, and without reserve, the position in which the course of events have placed me in reference to that Government, that I may submit to such judgment as you decide to be just and proper in my case.

I entered the Navy of the United States in 1841, having been appointed from my native State of North Carolina, and have discharged, I hope faithfully, all the duties assigned me. On the 11th of July, 1859, I was assigned to duty in the U. S. steamer Saginaw, ordered to China, and continued to discharge duty as a Lieutenant of that vessel, until the 15th day of December, 1860, when I was ordered to duty on board of the U. S. sloop of war John Adams, and continued to perform duty on board of the last named vessel until her return to New York on the 11th instant. The Civil War which now so unhappily distracts the Country, had not originated when I left the country, and on the 20th of November, 1861, so soon as by the newspapers I learned of its existence, I handed to the Commanding Officer of the John Adams, to be forwarded to the Navy Department, my resignation as an officer of the United States, which is now on file in that Department. On the arrival of the John Adams in New York, I took, under protest, the oath which was tendered me, that I might come to my family in this place, and have an opportunity of laying my case before your Excellency, for it is impossible that I could bear arms against the South in this war. All of my relations reside there, and my brothers are members of the Southern Army. As it is possible that I would have been placed in confinement if I had not taken the oath which I did take (under protest, and with the object before indicated of submitting the matter to your decision), I deem it due to my honor, that I should place my person at the disposal of the Government, as fully as it was prior to my taking the oath on my arrival at New York. I can be found in this place at any time.

Respectfully,
James I. Waddell.

I expected to be arrested from day to day, but was not; my communication was not noticed. The following speaks for itself.

COPY

Navy Department,
January 18, 1862.

Sir:

Your resignation as a Lieutenant in the Navy of the United States, tendered in your letter of the 20 November, 1861, has been received. By direction of the President, your name has, this day, been stricken from the rolls.

I am, respectfully, your obedient servant,

Gideon Welles.

Mr. James I Waddell,
Late Lieutenant, U. S. Navy,
New York.
(Commodore Paulding)
New York Navy Yard.


I received the above at Annapolis, Md. on the 28 January.


COPY

Treasury Department,
Fourth Auditor's Office,
February 1, 1862.

Sir:

In reply to your letter of the 20th instant, I would state that the Hon. Secretary of the Navy, under date of April 26, 1861, says, "The amounts found to be due resigned Navy Officers from the States which claim to have seceded, will hereafter be paid them from the U. S. funds heretofore sent to or deposited in those States, except in cases where the Department shall otherwise direct." Be pleased to inform me if you desire your amount settled in compliance with this order.

I am, Sir, respectfully, your obedient servant,

Hobart Barrian.

In reply to the above, I said if the Government will give me a pass to go South, I will endeavor to collect the money due me by the U.S. Government. The following official document is of the greatest importance. The Hon. Secretary of the Navy may have intended releasing me from every obligation; he certainly considered my letter to the President as undoing what had been exacted of me at New York in the shape of an oath; read and consider it for a moment.

*COPY*

Navy Department,
February 21, 1862.

Sir:

Your letter of the 15th instant, requesting that the Fourth Auditor be directed to settle your amount, has been received. In reply, you are informed that if you will address a communication to the Department, *engaging upon your word of honor,* to take no part in the war now being waged against the Government, your request will be complied with.

I am, respectfully, your obedient servant,

Gideon Welles.

Mr. Jas. I Waddell,
Annapolis, Md.

It was an attempt on the part of the Hon. Gideon Welles to bribe, and to confine his bribe to what was not his or the Government he represented. It was the reward of my labor,

70

it was my money, is my money yet, although the U.S. Government keeps possession of it; I hope whenever it is paid to me or mine, the Government will consider the honorable thing, and pay interest. After I had received [the] official letter of February 21, 1862, I began to arrange for my departure South. I had failed to get permission to collect my unsettled amount in Dixie, and I had neglected to make any promises to that debased official. My first arrangement was for a vessel to call at this port, Annapolis, at night, when I would go on board. That failed.

A friend informed me, if I wanted to get South, to visit Marsh Market, Baltimore, and enter said market at the south end, to the first beef stall on the right, approach and inquire of a fat man, "the price of beef."

I followed the directions and my fat friend's reply was, "Do you want to go South?"

"Yes."

"I will call for you tomorrow evening about eight o'clock and take you to Carroll Island. A schooner will be there to go to Virginia. Where shall I call?"

"Hoffman Street."

"No. ———."

I had arranged with a friend to meet me in Baltimore if I could find a way to go South. My Baltimore friend telegraphed to a friend in Annapolis, "Send that sample of tobacco," which telegram passed into my friend's hands, and he joined me a short time before I took leave of my wife and child.

We were taken to Carroll Island in a torrent of rain in a two-horse team, and on the journey the driver asked if I was in the vehicle. He said, handing me a small pellet in tinfoil, "Give that to Mr. Benjamin."

71

I took it and wondered who sent it and who could the driver be.

We reached Carroll Island at midnight, the rain still falling, and we drew up in front of a log cabin, half the roof tumbled in, and found ten persons waiting for the schooner.

I had paid the butcher one hundred dollars passage money for myself and friend. At daylight a schooner came to anchor and we boarded her, determined to press her into service and sail away for the sacred soil. The schooner was the right one, and her Yankee skipper was for money making, notwithstanding his love for the Union. When we reached the Potomac River, the McClelland fleet of steamboats were on the way for Washington City.

I recommended the people to go below, the skipper and myself remaining on deck. We had not yet reached the entrance to the Big Wycomico River, nor did we intend to enter that river while anything warlike was in sight.[9] Finally things looked clear. We pushed in and were favored with an east wind. We followed the channel by the stakes which were driven at intervals along its margin, but we had not pursued our course long, before a boat was seen advancing from the North bank. It had one sitter, and I hailed, "Are you a pilot?"

"Yes."

"Come alongside," and we waited for him and he came on board and informed us of a Federal cavalry force in West-

[9] Does Waddell mean the Potomac? If he entered the Wicomico in Maryland, he does not mention recrossing the bay to the west shore, which certainly would have been a hazardous wartime journey. Waddell probably landed somewhere on the south shore of the Potomac and traveled overland by wagon to the Rappahannock, where he crossed the river and went on to Richmond by rail.

moreland Co., and that he would take us to a place where we might safely leave the vessel.

We landed on the north side of a creek into which he had run the schooner, and I was delegated to visit a house near the spot of landing and learn the news.

There was naught about the house or its surroundings to indicate home. I reached the front door and waited for a reply to my rap. An old man of kind demeanor opened the door and said, "Friend or foe?"

"Friends," I replied.

"Come in friends."

I entered. The old man's wife sat at one corner of the fireplace, and a lad of 16 years sat at the other corner, dressed in a Confederate gray uniform, infantry.

I was in the act of stating my mission, when turning to address the old man, he said, "That boy is my grandson. He was in the battle of Bull Run and was sent home to die," and a big crystal tear rolled down his furrowed cheeks.

"We are old and alone. They can't hurt us. Our sons, all of them are gone. Some to return no more. Others in the army where they should be," and with that closing he braced himself up and looked like a man.

I then told him we wanted to get to Richmond, and could he not put us in the way to reach Rappahannock?

He furnished us with two vehicles to go as far as the village of ———, where we could hire wagons for the journey. We safely reached the village, and there we hired a wagon to take us to the ferry opposite Rappahannock.

Our driver was a Yankee and a Union man. We reached the ferry before sunset and found a guard boat, which ferried us to the other side of the Rappahannock River, where we were put in the guard house until the Commanding

Officer was apprised of our presence, who ordered the strangers to his quarters. We were accompanied to the hotel by an officer—a private of a Baltimore artillery company recognized us, and we were released and ate supper.

We proceeded in a wagon to a place on the York River Railroad, and were fortunate in meeting the train for Richmond. That evening we supped in the Spotswood hotel, and I delivered the tinfoil pellet to Mr. Benjamin.[10]

The following day we visited General Winder[11] and were recognized, and we visited the Navy Department and entered our applications for commissions in the Navy, similar to those we had relinquished in the Federal Navy.

I received my commission as a Lieutenant in the C.S. Navy, March 27, 1862.

The Zeft[12] brothers were employed in the construction of a ram at New Orleans. She was contracted for to be finished, and at the time I was ordered to her she was thought to be near completion. Farragut's fleet was threatening New Orleans, and it was very certain the Zefts [sic] could not finish, or even put the ram in a condition to be defended.

The enemy's fleet had passed the forts and defeated Hollins'[13] fleet of gunboats, and was steaming for New

[10] Judah P. Benjamin, then the Confederarcy's Attorney General, later its brilliant Secretary of State.

[11] General Winder was head of the Confederacy's secret service. This little-known man was Allan Pinkerton's counterpart in the South, but unlike Pinkerton, Winder was an impressive detective. In reading the unpublished memoirs of Pryce Lewis, the Pinkerton detective captured in Richmond, I found Winder to have been a highly efficient espionage leader.

[12] Tift Shipyards, New Orleans, the largest in the Confederacy. It built the first ironclad ship, the exploits of which proved to Mallory that iron rams held the secret to breaking the Union blockade.

[13] Captain George N. Hollins' gunboats were defeated in March, 1862. Hollins commanded the Mississippi River naval defenses. The defeat of his tiny fleet led to the subsequent battle of Fort Pillow.

74

Orleans. The naval officers and seamen were offered to the General commanding the land forces, to assist in the protection of the City, but the offer was declined.

A steamboat was then employed to convoy as far as Vicksburg, the naval people, and we all joined her. After leaving the ram, I volunteered to return in an open boat and destroy the ram. It seems the Naval Commander had forgotten that she could be destroyed, and it was agreed I should return and burn her. One man volunteered to go with me, and while I was standing on the deck of the ram, waiting for the man to report he had done his work, and was ready for inspection, mine having been completed earlier, five men came on board and asked if Zeft was there.

I told them no, then with an oath they cried out, "He is a traitor and we brought this rope to hang him."

I told them I had laid a train to the magazine, and the vessel would be fired in a few minutes. They retired quietly, and in a few minutes I fired her through, took my man in the open boat and regained the steamboat.

I returned to Richmond, and was ordered to Drury's Bluff[14] as Ordinance Officer, and was present when that brave man, Commodore John Rogers, was repulsed.

I was then ordered to report to the Navy Department, and with other officers, I was consulted as to the best manner of capturing the enemy's iron vessels, should they enter Charleston Harbor. This was so difficult a conundrum that I gave it up at once, and I answered the Secretary's conundrum by volunteering to attempt the capture after I had seen the monitors.

The senior officers evidently did not relish my volun-

[14] Drewry's Bluff.

teering, for one of them said, "We are all ready to volunteer."

I was ordered to Charleston and I was ordered by Lieutenant Webb, who was in command of what was then called "the forlorn hope" to organize the force, while he looked up steamboats, boats, etc. Colonel Kilt's Infantry regiment, thirteen hundred strong, and all of them voters in Kilt's congressional district, volunteered to fight the monitors single-handed. Kilt claimed to lead his men, and I told him I would be on his right. The monitors did not enter the Harbor, and I was ordered to Europe for foreign service, and I reached England in May, 1863.

# CHAPTER THREE

The iron-clads which the Messrs. Laird[15] were building were in rapid progress, and there was a reasonable hope they would be ready for service in autumn of 1863. It was, however, very doubtful if the British Government would allow the vessels to escape its vigilance, as did the Alabama, for those iron-clads had the capacity not only to raise the blockade of the Southern ports, but to enter the enemy's ports.[16]

Finally the vessels were seized. That hope vanished. An English company offered me the command of a blockade runner, and one thousand pounds for each round trip, to and from Bermuda, to any Southern port in the Confederacy.

I consulted Flag Officer Barron[17] and received his consent to accept the command. I slept on it and my wife asked me to decline the service. In a few days thereafter I was directed to hold myself in readiness for active service.

The British Government felt a serious responsibility would attach, should iron-clad vessels escape from their ports.

[15] Laird Brothers Shipyards, Brinkenham, across the Mersey River from Liverpool.

[16] The theory that the first targets of the rams were to be northern cities is no Sunday supplement story. Commander Bulloch, Charles Francis Adams, and Consul Dudley's detectives all testified to this. At the time, ram 294 was the largest iron battleship outside of Napoleon III's flagship. When the C.S.S. *Stonewall*, the one ram Bulloch did get to sea, arrived in Cuba en route to the east coast of the United States to pierce the blockade and attack northern cities, its skipper, Captain Thomas Jefferson Page, was notified of the end of the war. The *Stonewall* was then sold by Page to the Spaniards at Cuba for enough money to pay off the crew.

[17] Barron was one of Bulloch's principal agents. He was active not only in England but also in France and Scotland.

To check their career would be quite improbable with the enemy, and the destruction to property in the enemy's ports might lead to complications which England would avoid by holding the vessels. Wooden vessels of war were contracted for and built by agents for the Confederacy, and the reason why those vessels were finally seized, was because the success of the South had grown to be a very great doubt in the minds of men. I have mentioned a belief; from the fact that as the South had no seamen, it was unwise to buy or build fighting ships.

Where were the seamen to come from? True, poor Jack is marketable, but he is human, and did not like war better than other men, particularly in another man's fight.

I will say with pardonable modesty that had any number of vessels capable of carrying one gun, been purchased abroad by the Confederacy early in the war, they would have driven from the seas, or captured the merchant marine of the enemy. Our people had to meet and defend their territory against the enemy's advancing armies, but it was not war to engage the enemy on the ocean. It was war to avoid his power, and burn, sink and destroy his vessels. War is a trade, and should be governed by the rules of trade. If the South could have contested the supremacy of the ocean with the enemy, it would have been war. The brave conduct of Semmes was magnificent, but it was not war. The too great risk of getting to sea vessels of war, and the still greater risk in failing to get seamen for them, does not justify spending millions in that folly. The British Government prevented such war vessels from being got to sea, and its "foreign enlistment act" exercised a wholesome influence over her seamen.

78

Naval officers are generally very conservative men. They had nothing to do with the contest between the political elements of the North and the South. They were generally employed on foreign stations, and more than the officers of the other branch of the National defence, had lived under the flag as the visible embodiment of their country, and to this course may be ascribed the fact that more naval than army men remained with the North when their States seceded. These officers who had been placed, at an early age, upon the decks of vessels of war, enclosed by wooden walls in a floating prison, were educated under a stern and peculiar discipline to adapt them to a profession that required foreign, rather than home service, and which excluded them from all participation in the policy of government, and the internal interests of the country.

Those discussions which excited sectional discord and animosities among the people, exercised small influence upon the minds of naval officers. Their opinions on political questions were generally in condemnation of the doctrines set forth by noisy demagogues and wild theorists. With greater opportunity for observing the workings of other governments, they were more patient with the faults of their own. Their sympathies with the common country were wider and more universal and they sacrificed as much, if not more, than any other class of individuals, in espousing the Southern cause. It is well known with what regret they threw aside those emblems and decorations which linked boyish pleasure with manhood's pride, and which, from long association, had become necessary almost to their very existence.

The Federal flag was dear to them, but they were forced

to abandon it or sail beneath its folds to the <u>destruction</u> <u>of their homes and their kindred.</u>

The naval officers who followed the destiny of the South, could have been actuated by no selfish motive; no belief in rapid professional advancement prompted their withdrawal from the Federal service.

The South had no ships to encourage such ambition—no seamen; and it was apparent from the first, to all connected with that Government, that the battles would be fought on land and not at sea.[18] A pure and honest belief in the allegiance due to their respective States alone influenced those men. Dear to them as was the old flag and old associations, they felt it impossible to retain position under a Government repudiated by the people whom they served, and to whom they were united by the strongest ties which unite man to man, the ties of kindred blood. Rather than be inactive, the naval officers of the South went into the army as engineers and gunners. They were thus employed at Vicksburg, along the Mississippi River [and] at Drury's Bluff upon the James River [and] at temporary structures on the Potomac, and the rivers farther south; in Mobile and elsewhere, their energy and intelligence led them into machine shops and arsenals.

In one of these, the invention of Lieutenant Brooke for plating with iron, vessels of war, was developed, and his improvement in gunnery and ordnance, were perfected.

These officers planned expeditions to harrass [sic] the enemy, and volunteered to lead attacking parties in the Chesapeake Bay and Potomac River, where Lieutenant

18 At the outbreak of the war the Confederacy had only one fighting ship, the C.S.S. *Sumter*.

Wood, Pelot, Hogue and others destroyed or captured the enemy's armed vessels, leading our fearless and impetuous men in open boats against fearful odds.[19]

The naval contest in Hampton Roads, Mobile Bay, and on the waters of the Mississippi, have placed upon the brows of all those noble spirits who participated in them a wreath of imperishable glory. It was only after forcible representations to the Government, that a few vessels were purchased and sent to sea in search of the enemy's commerce.

The intense anxiety of every patriotic sailor to share the perils of the contest with his countrymen may be easily conceived. They were impatient to lift from their heads the odium their inaction brought upon them, and to give to the people of the South evidence of their fitness for daring and enterprise. During the first year of the war, Lieutenants Pegram and Sinclair urged the Government to send vessels to the Pacific Ocean in search of the enemy's commerce, but the idea was considered impracticable.

Naval officers urged the importance of attacking the enemy's commerce at every turn, indicated the most vulnerable points of assault, and discountenanced building fighting vessels in foreign countries. The capitalists of the North could only be reached through the destruction of Atlantic commerce; their attack would draw off cruisers from the Southern ports, so that a reduced number on service could not

[19] Waddell is referring to the small band of young officers who attacked and captured several steamers on the Chesapeake and Potomac. One of the most colorful was a handsome young officer who masqueraded as a woman. He is known to naval history as "the French Lady." His never before published story will be incorporated in a volume on the Civil War being prepared by the author.

watch so closely the Southern blockade runners which brought to us war material and the necessities of life.

With what impatience we burned to enter upon this duty may be easily imagined, and with what delight the writer received from his superior officer a summons to a confidential conference can be well understood. The following letter of instructions was placed in his hands.

> Paris, France, 5 October, 1864,
> No. 30, Rue Drouot.

Sir:

When the vessel under your command is ready for sea, you will sail on a cruise in a region of ocean already indicated to you in our personal interviews. The charts which have been sent you, are the best sailing directions which you can have.

Your position is an important one, not only with reference to the immediate results to the enemy's property, but from the fact that neutral rights may frequently arise under it; reliance, however, is placed in your judgment and discretion for meeting and promptly disposing of such questions.

It is now quite the custom of Federal owners of ships and cargoes to place them under British protection, and this may at times cause you embarrassment. The strictest regard for the rights of neutrals cannot be too sedulously observed; nor should an opportunity be lost in cultivating friendly relations with their naval and merchant services, and of placing the true character of the contest in which we are engaged in its proper light. You will not hesitate to assume responsibility when the interest of your country may demand it, and should your judgment ever hesitate in seeking the solution of any difficulty, it may be aided by the reflection that you are to do the enemy's property the greatest injury in the shortest time. Authority is vested in you to make acting appointments to fill any vacancies which may occur.

The maintenance of strict naval discipline will be essential to your success, and you will enjoin this upon your officers and enforce its rigid observance, always tempering justice with humane and kind treatment.

I am, Sir, very respectfully, your obedient servant,

S. Barron,
Flag Officer.

Lieutenant Commanding James I. Waddell.


Received from Navy Department, Richmond, dated August 19, 1864, and enclosed in a letter of instructions to Lieutenant Commanding James I. Waddell, dated October 5, 1864.

A fast vessel with auxiliary steam power, leaving the meridian of the Cape of Good Hope on the first of January, would reach Sydney in Australia in forty days, adding twenty days for incidental interruptions, and leaving the coast of Australia on the first of March, passing through the whaling ground between New Zealand and New Holland, and the Caroline Group, touching at Ascension, and allowing 30 days for incidental interruptions, would reach the Ladrone Islands by the first of June. She would then, visiting the Bonin Islands, Sea of Japan, Okhotsk Sea and North Pacific, be in position, about the 15th of September, north of the Island of Oahu, distant from sixty to one hundred miles, to intercept the North Pacific Whaling fleet, bound to Oahu with the products of the summer cruise.


I was ordered to proceed upon a cruise in the far distant Pacific, into the seas and among the islands frequented by the great whaling fleet of New England, a source of abundant wealth to our cruisers and a nursery for her seamen, and it was hoped that I would be able to damage and disperse the fleet, even if I did not succeed in utterly destroying it.

Considering the vast extent of water to be sailed over, the necessarily incomplete equipment of the vessel and my approaching isolation from the aid of my countrymen, a letter of specific instructions would have been wholly superfluous.

All details regarding the organization of the crew and the necessary alterations required to fit the vessel for carrying her battery, preserving the ammunition, the general conduct of the cruise and my intercourse with neutrals was left to my judgment and discretion, for I would be subjected to constantly varying scenes and incidents, and would doubtless encounter difficulties which could not be foreseen and provided for in advance.

I believe that in moments of doubt and difficulty the conscientious officer who is earnestly intent upon his duty, finds that a happy inspiration comes to his aid. Upon that I relied as I dwelt upon my letter of instruction, not yet knowing who were the officers of the ship with whom I was to be associated, upon whose experience and ability depended in a great measure the success of the great work to be accomplished.

I had the benefit of the counsel, wisdom and experience of my superior officer in all matters connected with the projected cruise, the probable difficulties in the way and their solution. Indeed, the way was paved for my operations so skillfully that there was little else to do but follow the instructions given me.

The means which were to be placed at my disposal, and the arrangement for a proper and safe rendezvous, the process of transferring the armament and stores from the supply vessel to the intended cruiser, and the probable nature of the contract with the seamen to induce them to ship in our service, were matters of after consideration.

The passage to my ultimate cruising ground and the locality in which I would be most likely to find the objects of my search required careful study and investigation of charts and reference to the topography of the Pacific Ocean and the numerous islands scattered therein. The ultimate aim of the cruise was the dispersion or utter destruction of the New England whaling fleet, as pointed out in the memorandum of the Secretary of the Navy. The vessel to be placed under my command had recently returned from her first voyage to Bombay[20] for which trade she was built, and being designed as a transport for troops going to or returning from India with spacious 'tween decks and large air ports, she was admirably suited for being converted into a cruising vessel.

The log of her outward and homeward voyages showed her to be fast under canvas, and her steam power was more than auxiliary. She had been docked for the purpose of examining her condition before entering upon a cruise. She had a lifting screw and she could steam nine knots under favorable circumstances. Ample stores were provided for a cruise of fifteen months. The following named officers were detailed for my command:

| | |
|---|---|
| William C. Whittle | Lieutenant |
| John Grimball | " |
| Francis T. Chew | " |
| S. Smith Lee | " |

[20] The *Sea King*. Ten months before, Bulloch had spotted this "beautiful ship" in Glasgow, but she had sailed before his broker could buy her. On his second tour of Europe's waterfronts, seeking ships, the broker saw the *Sea King*.

| | |
|---|---|
| Dabney M. Scales | Lieutenant |
| Charles E. Lining | Passed Assistant Surgeon |
| F. J. McNulty | "          " |
| Irvine S. Bulloch | Acting Master[21] |
| O. A. Brown | Midshipman |
| J. T. Mason | " |

We left Liverpool in search of the cruiser in the Confederate supply vessel Laurel, on the morning of the 9th of October, 1864, for Funchal, Island of Madeira.

A few picked men selected from the crew of the late Confederate States steamer Alabama, who were specially retained, accompanied us and constituted the nucleus of the force which we should have to organize at the place of rendezvous.

Among the men was George Harwood, the chief boatswain's mate of the late Alabama, a good seaman, an experienced man-of-wars man, and one calculated to carry weight and influence with a crew composed exclusively of foreigners. It was determined to give him an appointment of acting boatswain as soon as the supply vessel was clear of the channel and to explain to him with what intention we left England. We were sure he would assist materially in persuading the men intended for the cruiser to reship for our service. For obvious reasons there should be, after reaching Funchal, as little communication with the shore as possible. None of the officers or men would be allowed to land; every precaution would be observed to prevent information reaching the shore of the character of our visit and the destination of the cruise.

From the time we separated from our supply vessel, and

[21] This was the nephew of Commander Bulloch, the Naval Agent.

after her arrival at Nassau, everything would necessarily be known, but by that time we should be far on our cruise and beyond the reach of interference. The object in taking the supply vessel to Funchal was to place ourselves and the naval stores on board of the intended cruiser, and that she might attend upon us until we were fairly in possession. Consequently her commander was directed to shape the movements of his vessel in accordance with my wishes and only proceed to carry out his special instructions when we no longer needed his assistance.

The amount of stores to be transferred was not large. The heaviest weight in a single piece was less than three tons. The trans-shipment might easily be accomplished within twenty-four hours, if the weather proved favorable, in which case the two vessels could be lashed alongside of each other with fenders to prevent rubbing and chafing and by steaming slowly ahead with one, so as to tow the other, and keeping well under the lea of the Island of Madeira, the transfer might be accomplished without the delay and risk of seeking anchorage.

# CHAPTER FOUR

The Alabama supplies were taken on board while underway off the Island of Terceira, but should the state of the weather prevent the above named course, I should have to consider where to seek a rendezvous, and to that matter an abundance of thought was devoted.

An essential point to be considered was the final destination of the supply vessel and her ability to reach it without drawing upon our supply of coal. On the coast of Morocco are the roadsteads of Magador, Saffi[22] and Cape Ghir, but those are unsafe anchorages, with bad holding ground even in summer, and at that season (the autumn) the westerly swell of the Atlantic, to which they are exposed, would not permit the vessels to lie together in contact.

The same objections held good with regard to Teneriffe and Palmos[23] in the Grand Canaries, and any point farther south, although in the direction of our cruising ground would take the supply vessel too far away from her intended port.

I was advised not to lose time in looking up doubtful places of resort on that side of the Atlantic, should weather off Madeira prove too unfavorable for operations, my attention was directed to the Caicoș Group in the West Indies, which lie between the 15th and 22nd parallels of north latitude, and are nearly bisected by the 72nd meridian of west longitude.

[22] Mogador, Safi.
[23] Las Palmas.

88

Here I was sure of still water and safe anchorage and there would be no interference or danger of entanglement for breach of neutrality.

At the Caicos Group there are two anchorages, one under West Caicos Islands, and the other at South Caicos Islands, called Cockburn Harbor.

If anything should prevent my using either or both these anchorages, we could run upon the Silver Bank, close under the rocks marked "Awash." In that neighborhood we could be able to transfer supplies and the supply vessel could run up through Emma Sound[24] and into Nassau, where those persons who might decline to ship for service in the intended cruiser could be landed and forwarded by steamer to England.

Some skill would be necessary in dealing with the men and persuading them to ship. We knew that this would be greatly facilitated by the influence of the Alabama's men who were willing to serve. It was therefore desirable to throw them on board of the cruiser and in communication with her crew at the earliest possible moment, and let them be brought over by quiet influence during the time we ran for a rendezvous.

The monthly pay lawfully allowed to seamen in the navy was not sufficient to tempt men to serve in our cruisers and they fully understood our position and looked for strong inducements to ship.

Seamen, as far as our service was concerned, were merchantable articles with a market value. It was necessary to pay the price demanded or dispense with their services and abandon the cruise. It was felt, therefore, that if, in the

[24] Exuma Sound into Nassau.

exercise of my discretion, it became necessary to go beyond the established pay allowance, the Navy Department would take steps necessary to legalize the act.

An unusually large crew was shipped for the supply vessel, and an exertion would be made to persuade as many of them as could be spared to ship for the intended cruiser. From the united crews of both vessels we hoped to be able to engage fifty who, with the ten from the Alabama, would make a crew of sixty, and these added to the officers would be a sufficient number to navigate the vessel with ease and safety, and even to fight the guns, and this force could be steadily supplemented from prizes and from the first island we touched at where whalers rendezvous.

The supply vessel reached Madeira the 16th day of October, 1864, and was anchored in Funchal Bay near Loo Rock.

On the following day orders were given that there would be no communication with the shore except that which was necessary for the commander of the supply vessel in his intercourse with the custom officials and for purchase of coal for the vessel. A lookout was stationed to report the appearance of all vessels coming in sight off the harbor, and to report such arrivals day and night, and if any passing vessel hoisted flags or showed lights, to inform the commander of the supply vessel or, in his absence from the vessel to inform me of the character of such signals and the general appearance of the vessel.

The supply vessel received all the coal she required, and inquiries were made of her commander by inquisitive people about her destination and the passengers who strolled about her decks.

During the first watch on a clear, calm, moonlight night, (such as generally blessed that happy group of islands) on the 18th of October, 1864, a ship-rigged vessel came in sight within two miles of Funchal steaming slowly and showed signal lights, which is not an unusual courtesy for vessels to extend to those lying in the anchor. The object of such civility is an announcement of the vessel's name and tidings of her safety, in order that they may be communicated to those interested in her voyage. Marriot's code of signals furnishes all English and nearly all American names of vessels, and by referring to this work when vessels communicate by signals, their names, character and cargoes together with the port from which and to which they are bound can be known.

This vessel excited great interest among us. She soon passed out of sight south of the port [Funchal] and soon returned off the port [port side], steaming slowly in the direction from whence she came, still showing her signal lights, which the crews of other vessels in the harbor did not appear to notice. It was impossible just then to leave port in order to communicate with the stranger. The commander of the supply vessel had not received his papers from the custom officials and while he was communicating this fact to me, the black craft went back north of the port and was hidden from view. Her advent had caused no small stir among the crew of the supply vessel who were assembled on deck in merry chat and to avoid the confined air below. And when she again came in sight, a low suppressed exclamation of "that's her," escaped the lips of the men who were hanging over the ship's rail eagerly watching the strange steamer, and who had by this time some suspicion of what we were looking for.

After the disappearance of the steamer we all withdrew from the deck of the Laurel, some to sleep, others to talk over their suspicions as to the character of the long, low, black craft, and their fate in connection with hers, and all longed for the morning light with its developments. The papers of all vessels are deposited after arrival at the custom house. It is a guarantee of character, a security for payment of custom dues and the observance of port regulations.

Daylight came, the sun rose bright and warm. A messenger was despatched for a customs official to repair on board with the ship's papers, and while the custom boat was being pulled off to the Laurel accompanied by bum-boats and fishing smacks whose purpose it is to coax the last farthing out of thriftless Jack, that strange steamer came in sight again from the north with signals flying from her mast heads, evidently meaning business, which were recognized and answered from the Laurel and a cry arose from the shore boats which surrounded her "otro Alabama, otro Alabama." The fires had been kindled at daylight so that the steam was ready. Chain was in to a short stay, the Laurel swung rapidly, and we were all impatient to follow the stranger and ascertain her wants, whose symmetrical outlines the glorious sun now played fairly upon and she appeared to be the very object of my search for which I had left Liverpool.

The custom of officials being settled with and all strangers seen out of the steamer the anchor was tripped at 10 A.M., and we stood to sea in chase of the steamship, whose engines were slowed to enable the Laurel to overhaul her quickly.

The 19th day of October, 1864 was fine and the wind blew from southwest. So soon as the Laurel drew near the steamship I saw on her port quarter three words in large white letters, Sea King, London.

Each of us asked himself instinctively, what great adventures shall we meet in her? What will be her ultimate fate? The Sea King was directed to follow her consort, and together we sought reference on the north side of the Desertas, where we found smooth sea and good anchorage.

Mr. William C. Whittle, Jr., Lieutenant and Executive Officer of my command, joined us from the Sea King.

## List of Acting Appointments

| | | |
|---|---|---|
| Matthew O'Brien | Acting Chief Engineer | Louisiana |
| W. H. Codd | " First Asst. " | Maryland |
| W. Breedlove Smith | " Assistant Paymaster | Louisiana |
| Fred J. McNulty | " " Surgeon | Connecticut |
| George Harwood | " Boatswain | England |
| John Lynch | " Carpenter | New York |
| Henry Alcot | " Sailmaker | England |
| John L. Guy | " Gunner | England |

## Petty Officers

| | | |
|---|---|---|
| Joshua T. Minor | Acting Master's Mate | Virginia |
| Lodge Cotton | " " " | Maryland |
| C. E. Hunt[25] | " " " | Virginia |

All acting master's Mates were in the Confederate naval service, first class petty officers.

The Shenandoah, late the Sea King, was commissioned on the ocean the 19th day of October, 1864, under the lee and on the north side of the islands known as the Desertas, a few miles from the island of Madeira. She was anchored in 18 fathoms and the Laurel came to and was lashed along-

---

[25] Hunt published his experiences the following year.

side of her. The little nook was smooth, the day bright and cheering, and we felt it a harbinger of success.

In thirteen hours after we were on the deck the consort had safely discharged all stores intended for the Shenandoah, and was only waiting for such passangers as she was compelled to receive on board. Our deck was crowded with every conceivable outfit. Confusion reigned supreme, and we realized the almost endless labor before us, but we had every encouragement in the consciousness that we had a good and fast ship under our feet, and courageous hearts to sail her. There was a quantity of work inside as well as outside of her to be done, and to accomplish all that a crew was the first necessity, and it became my effort to ship the crew of the late Sea King and as many of the crew of the Laurel as possible. The men were therefore called to the quarter deck of the Shenandoah, when I informed them of the changed character of the Sea King, read my commission to them, pictured to them a brilliant, dashing cruise, and asked them to join the service of the Confederate States and assist an oppressed and brave people in their resistance to a powerful and arrogant northern government. Only twenty-three men were willing to venture on such service, and a majority of those shipped for six months. Those who declined to serve in the Shenandoah were directed to go on board the Laurel.

Our feeble force was then ordered to get the anchor which proved too heavy and the officers threw off their coats and assisted in lifting it to the bow, and the little adventurer entered upon her watchful career, throwing to the breeze the flag of the South, and demanding for her a place among her sister nations upon that vast expanse of water. Lieutenant Chew effaced the words Sea King from

94

the stern of the Shenandoah. Our flag unfolded itself gracefully to the freshening breeze and declared the majesty of the country it represented, saluted by the cheers of a handful of brave hearted men who stood upon our deck and acclamations from the Laurel that was steaming away for the land we love, to tell the tale to those who would rejoice that another cruiser was afloat and who would share the triumph or reverses which might befall her.

We were now fairly afloat in a vessel of 1100 tons, English measurement, constructed for peaceful pursuits but metamorphosed into an armed cruiser.[26] The deck had to be cleared of the stores pitched on it pell mell before the battery could be mounted on the carriages and gunports must be cut, fighting belts driven, gun tackle fitted, before that battery could be used in our defense. All this service which is ordinarily done at a navy yard before a vessel is commissioned devolved upon us, out in mid ocean, without even a hope of successful defense or a friendly port to take shelter in, if attacked in the interim.

The carpenter of the vessel could find no one who was capable of assisting him in his department. He therefore unassisted, was to make the necessary alterations and of course, the work would progress slowly.

Besides the work already mentioned, the bulwarks were discovered to be too weak for resistance to a shotted gun,

[26] Bulloch's official measurements of the Shenandoah are as follows: "She is 1160 tons, classed A-1 for fourteen years at Lloyds; frames, beams, etc., of iron but planked from keel to gunwale with East India teak. She is a full rigged ship with rolling top sails, has plenty of accommodations for officers of all grades. Her 'tween decks' are 7 ft. 6 in. with large air ports. Her engines are direct acting with two cylinders 47 inches in diameter, 2 ft. 9 in. stroke, nominal horsepower 220 but indicating 850 horsepower and she has a lifting screw. The log of the ship shows her to be a fast sailor under canvas for with her screw up she has made 330 miles in 24 hours."

and therefore some plan must be devised for strengthening them, which being decided upon and arranged, the next work of importance was the selection of a place in the vessel's hold where a powder magazine could be built.

The hold as well as half of the berth deck was filled with coal and not being able to move the coal from the forehold which was selected as the place for the magazine, the powder was placed under tarpaulins in my starboard cabin, while I occupied the port one. Was it not a warm companion?

If we had fallen in with the enemy's cruiser at this time we might, in attempting to escape, have received a missile which, taking effect in the stern of the vessel, would have exploded or otherwise put an end to all our hopes, by blowing up the magazine. There was, however, no other place at that time so safe for the powder as the cabin where we had twenty-four officers, each department having its complement, making all told forty-seven persons.

### List of Acting Appointments

| John Hutchinson | Acting | Second | Assistant | Engineer | Scotland |
| Earnest Muggufrey | " | Third | " | " | Ireland |

The novel character of my position embarrassed me more than the feeble condition of my command. I had the compass to guide us as seamen but my instructions made me a magistrate in a new field of duty where the law was not very clear even to lawyers. To manage a vessel in stormy weather and exposure to the danger of the sea, was a thing for which every good sailor was competent. Fighting was a profession we had prepared ourselves for but now I was to sail and fight and to decide questions of international law that lawyers had quarreled over with all their books. I was in all matters to act promptly and without counsel, but my admirable instructions and those principles of honor and patriotism which animated every southern gentleman gave me that confidence which supported me amidst all the difficulties and responsibilities of the situation.

# CHAPTER FIVE

The Shenandoah was a composite built ship, i.e., her frame was of iron, and her hull of wood, six inches teak. Her lower and topsailyards and bowsprit were iron, her horse power 180. Her cylinders were five feet and her boilers 18 inches above the water line. She was capable of condensing 500 gallons of water and consuming twenty tons of coal per day when steaming. I never saw her exceed ten knots per hour under steam alone.[27] She was very fast under sail, very dry, and easy upon her spars. She was a pretty craft in every position. She appeared to be oversparred but she was not. The topsail yards were so heavy that if it were not for winches introduced into the merchant-service for lifting heavy bodies, I really do not believe the crew could have mast headed the topsail. The power of the entire force was hardly equal to lifting so heavy an iron spar, and yet if that spar had been wood it would have been heavier. The running gear was generally so damaged it became necessary to reeve anew and as seamen will never neglect their ship because fine weather may be expected, a general overhauling was inaugurated and everybody was set to work.

When the helmsman was wanted elsewhere I would steer the ship. Of the number of men who shipped, five were found fitted for the engineer department. Such disposition of service between the deckhands and the engineer depart-

[27] It is doubtful that any sea dog would have used this expression. Probably a landlubber typist.

98

ment as would conduce to health and good understanding became a subject for consideration and I determined, as it was all important, to run the vessel as quickly as possible away from the place of rendezvous and to seek lighter winds and a smoother sea for operations, to keep the ship under steam during daylight, and after dark to stop the engines, put the ship under canvas and change the course for the night.

The wind was free; the course was southward; and as the breeze freshened after night, the ship made per hour under sail as much as she did during the day under steam. The watch was seldom disturbed during the night, for the ship was under short sail to prevent their being called.

The Shenandoah was furnished with Enfield rifles, cutlasses and revolvers, and on the deck in huge boxes lay the guns and carriages. Though impatient to see the guns mounted and their grim mouths projecting beyond our wooden walls, of what use could they be in defense of so vulnerable a vessel? To be sure their appearance would go a long way towards intimidating an unarmed vessel but very little examination showed clearly our utter incapacity for contending with any show of success against a regularly appointed man-of-war steamer, but the enemy did not know that.

I determined to take the offensive immediately. That is the only way for the feeble to act towards a strong foe. It may be called audacity, but it is pluck, and your foe knows he may be hurt some way, and that very respect it engenders is very often the safeguard.

The deck was cleared of such articles as belonged below, the gun boxes lashed to and near the sides where the ports were destined to be cut, and having a partially clear deck, we could, with the aid of an Enfield rifle, make ourselves known to every one we met, and should they prove to be the kind we were in search of, appropriate them.

The crew was not sufficiently numerous to manage the vessel easily, and unless we found the enemy's vessels and succeeded not only in capturing them but in shipping a part of their respective crews, our own men might become disheartened and the cruise fail. Work is not congenial to Jack's nature. He is essentially a loafer, and we apprehended that captured men coming on board would judge for themselves of the ship's condition, and a bad impression might be made which it would be difficult to correct.

We could rely on our men using rough arguments with those who were undecided, and we felt sure that each prize would have in its crew one or more adventurous spirits, and we wanted none others, who would avail of the opportunity we would offer them in hope of prize money, and under the assurance of being well cared for.

The sailor appreciates kindness from an officer, and is not apt to forget it, and although he wastes his money on shore, he is a close and penurious rascal on shipboard.

I have a strong regard for my brother professionals, whether before the mast or on the quarter-deck, and as I have been through the mill, I have a right to be heard. On the 22nd day of October, four days after I had commissioned the vessel, the guns were all on their carriages. Never was there better official material than I had associated with me.

The officers leading the men had accomplished a vast deal of labor and set so grand an example of devotion, energy and industry that Jack, if flagging a little at times, imbibed a new inspiration and contended with his leader for the most difficult job or the heaviest lift. The carpenter who had been assisted by Lieutenant Lee (Lee was jack of all trades), had succeeded in discovering a man who could lend him a hand in the work before him and Lee went at something else, never idle. Two ports were cut on either side of the deck. Other ports were to be cut and the fighting bolts were first to be found, before they could be driven. By some strange accident they escaped the observation of the gunner and were found a few days after in a beef barrel, stowed with provisions in the hold. Who would even look for fighting bolts in an empty beef barrel? And now the gun tackles could not be found, and it soon became a matter of certainty they never were put on board. We had plenty of rope, but no blocks suitable for gun tackles. The absence of them rendered the battery totally useless and the enemy must supply our wants.

I had been directed to live on his supplies, and I suppose gun tackles were embraced in those directions.

The guns were on their carriages, and as the gun tackles could not then be found, the carriages were secured fore and aft the deck, close to the ship's side, and in the absence of bolts, straps were passed through the scuppers and toggled outside to which the guns were lashed.

The deck then became more ship shape and the work was nearly completed above as far as we could proceed with it.

There was hard work below, for it was necessary to know what had been put in the vessel before we took charge of her, and it really seemed as if our labor would never end.

Several officers slept on the deck in the absence of berths, and wash deck buckets were resorted to in the place of basins. The furniture in my cabins consisted of one broken arm chair, one covered with velvet (cotton), no berth or lockers or bureau, no place to put clothing, no washstand, pitcher or basin; as cheerless a spot as ever the sun shone on.

The apartments assigned to the commissioned officers were in better condition, and as to the apartment for steerage officers, it was filled with iron tanks holding bread, and there was no furniture of any description for it. Notwithstanding these discomforts, we made merry over our situation. The enemy must supply deficiencies. Such were my directions. Poor John Yank, a great deal was expected from his commissary department. He, however, kept faithfully to our expectations, for we always had a Joe Hooker to fall back upon in any and every emergency,

The captain was the only anxious person on board. If amused for a moment by the cheerful tones of the officers, his thoughts would go back to the nature of the command and the important interests confided to him. It was my first command. Nobody ever had just such a one before, for upon the accuracy of all the calculations of my judgment depended success or failure.

On the 25th of October the powder was removed to a small apartment under the cabin, the deck of which was very little below the surface of the ocean, and divided from the steerage deck by a strong, open lattice work, which was rendered more secure against draughts by heavy canvas tacked to the partition. The powder was better protected there than in my cabin, but still in a very insecure place. Great caution was observed in guarding against accident. It would be impossible to enumerate the variety of work which had been done and that yet remained to be done in making the alterations necessary to convert a perfectly equipped merchant steamer into a national cruiser, and only those who have done such work on a broad and friendless ocean can appreciate the anxieties accompanying such a task.

An accident occurred to the machinery which did not improve the situation of affairs. The derangement was, however, corrected in a few hours and the engine put in motion again, but not without awakening doubts in the minds of the crew as to the durability of the machine.

By the 26th of October enough coal was removed from the berthdeck to fill the side bunkers, from which a supply had been drawn for steaming since the 19th instant. The removal of such a quantity of coal developed a large, spacious and finally ventilated deck upon which it was designed to berth the crew, and the coal which could not be placed in the side bunkers just then was thrown well aft on that deck.

The space occupied by the coal could be staped[28] for athwartships bunker without encroaching upon the quarters required for a full ship's company. After examination of the total area, it was found that there was ample room to berth 200 men comfortably, exclusive of that portion converted into a coal bunker, and the complement of men for the Shenandoah was fixed at 120.

On either side of the berth deck were metal lattice openings for ventilating to the hold, through which the gases would escape. A constant circulation of healthy air poured in at the air ports and hatches to the berthdeck, keeping up a wholesome change. This deck was seven and a half feet below the spar deck. The ship had now reached a low latitude and was constantly receiving heavy rain and violent

[28] An old English or Scottish word, now obsolete, meaning "stave" as in cask or tub. In other words, Waddell meant the coal had to be propped up by means of staves.

squalls of wind and, to our horror, the decks leaked like sieves, and the seams of the hull were sufficiently open to admit a fine spray from a sea which had spent itself on her sides.

On the 27th of October the little wanderer took the offensive and entered upon her first chase. In compliment to the stranger she was in pursuit of, she crossed for the first time the royal yards and rapidly overhauled her, which proved to be the Mogul of London.

Immediately after separating from that vessel she entered upon another chase and overhauled the ship as quickly. She too was British.

A seaman is never satisfied as to the sailing capacity of his ship until she is in company with other vessels, and the evidence obtained under such circumstances is not to be mistaken. The Shenandoah was unquestionably a fast vessel, and I felt assured it would be a difficult attempt to find her superior under canvas in a strong working breeze or ordinary wind. Give her the wind and steam need not be considered. The crews of those vessels rushed to their respective rails and three times three the red flag of old England dipped in salutation to the flag of the South. The Shenandoah had now reached a position where vessels from the westward on an outward voyage would probably be found, and our prospects brightened as we worked our way toward the line, through light and variable winds, sunshine and rain. The Mogul of London was an American built vessel and like many other American vessels, had changed owners in consequence of the war. She may have been sold in good faith. So far as her papers were concerned, the sale was in form, but that is not infallible proof.

On the 30th of October we chased, captured and scuttled

American bark Alena of Searsport, bound for Buenos Ayres [*sic*], with railroad iron. She was on her first voyage, perfectly equipped, nicely coppered, and reported by the boarding officer to be beautifully clean. There are no people who understand the building and equipment of vessels so well as the Yankee shipwright.

She was a valuable capture, furnishing the blocks for the gun tackles, a variety of blocks which the steamer was in want of and cotton canvas so very suitable for sail making. The officers partly fitted themselves out with basins, pitchers, mess crockery, knives, forks, etc. A spring bottom mattress fell to my share, and a small supply of provisions was removed to our ship. The crew saved all their luggage. They evidently anticipated some unpleasant treatment. They roamed about the deck uncertain what to do. Engaging in conversation with our men was but a prelude to an enlistment of their sympathies in our cause.

Five seamen and a coal passer entered their names on the shipping articles, and the crew then numbered twenty-nine. It was fortunate that our first capture could be settled, for the steamer's position was good and a bonfire would have given alarm to all Yankees within thirty miles, and then, too, any Federal cruiser which might have been in our neighborhood would have been attracted by the red glare of the sky and might have interfered with my movements.

The Alena was a valuable prize. The manner of destroying a prize depends on the character of her cargo. If freighted like the Alena, knock a hole in her bottom from in board below the water line and the vessel sinks rapidly and finally disappears leaving only a few pieces of plank floating over the great abyss which has closed over her.

It more frequently occurs that to destroy a prize, fire must be resorted to, and there is no escape from that ruthless element. However much it may be condemned, it is better than to leave a prize so disabled and injured as to be formidable enough to endanger the navigation of the ocean. Fire serves as a beacon to inform the sailor of danger, but it leaves a small portion of the vessel, the floor and the keel to float upon the surface of the water.

To prepare a vessel for destruction by fire, first remove all living animals, take out all useful equipment which may be wanted, discover what combustibles are in her hold, such as tar, pitch, turpentine, and see to the removal of gunpowder. All of these things should be thrown into the sea. Combustibles are then scattered throughout the vessel, bulkheads torn down and piled up in her cabins and forecastle. All hatches are opened and all halyards let go that the sails may hang loosely and the yards counter braced. Fire is then taken from the galley or cooking stove and deposited in various parts of her hold and about her deck.

If she is very old she burns like tinder. This painful duty which sometimes became necessary would have been avoided had we been allowed to take our prizes into port for adjudication.

Our first capture produced a marked difference in the bearing of the crew. The work pressed heavily still upon them, but we were now gathering strength in numbers from our captives and the cry of Sail ho! was greeted with manifestations of joy. After working hours, those who desired amusement collected in the gangways and gave themselves up to dancing, jumping, singing, or spinning yarns, in which the narrator was the hero.

Jack is easily entertained and simple in his tastes. The

course was still southward under the bright rays of a tropical sun which showed itself alternately between the showers of rain which wet our jackets. Jack says that rain water is very wet, which expression doubtless originated in his experience of the fact that salt water never produces cold from bathing or from a tumble into it, whereas he dreads fresh water.

On the 5th of November, we chased, captured and burned the schooner Charter Oak, (Gilmer, master,) of Boston, bound for San Francisco with a mixed cargo.

She was supplied with preserved fruits and a few excellent cabin stores, which were appropriated to our use. Two thousand pounds of canned tomatoes were brought on board, with other delicacies intended for cabin use.

Her captain, his wife and her widowed sister with her little son occupied my starboard cabin. Their personal effects were respected, and they messed at the same table with me and wardroom officers. The widow had lost her husband at Harper's Ferry. He had been a sergeant in the Federal army. The captain said he had only two hundred dollars in currency, and I believe him to have told the truth. When his wife came on board I presented her with the money in the presence of Midshipman Mason, on behalf of the Confederacy, on condition she would not give any part of it to her husband.

We all felt a compassion for these poor women, and we had no idea of retaliating upon them for the injuries which General Hunter, Sheridan, Sherman and their kind had inflicted on our unhappy countrywomen. A statement made by this Captain in some New York paper testifies to the kindess he received while he was a prisoner.

The crew of the Charter Oak consisted of a mate and

three Portuguese sailors. During the examination of their luggage United States Army overcoats were found and it turned out that these Portuguese were deserters from the Federal army, perhaps belonging to that class known as "bounty jumpers."

A sword found on board of her was the only trophy we preserved. The fate of this remains hereafter to be told. We received no aid in men from this crew.

It was interesting to witness the meeting between the two captive shippers under such strange circumstances. Their thoughts were in the same channel. There was no consolation to be offered them except the promise to send them home as soon as possible. The Searsport Yankee had lost money, while the Californian, after a few grimaces, took his capture as a good joke. They did not remain friends long as the Californian found the Yankee "agin his taste."

The Charter Oak was fired late in the afternoon and, to satisfy ourselves that she would be consumed, it was necessary for us to remain near her for a few hours after night. The wind was light and the bright flames from the hull, taking in succession each sail, followed the masts to their very trucks, so that the red glare could be seen a long way off, and was a signal of accidental fire or the work of a Confederate cruiser. In either case it would draw assistance.

The Charter Oak was of small value compared with the Alena. I ran the Shenandoah to leeward of the burning wreck and sufficiently distant from danger of taking fire.

An enemy, if in that region of ocean, would be under sail, or if under steam, would run his vessel first to windward to view the burning vessel when I could have been off without his perceiving us.

The gunports were now all cut, the guns were in position

or out to battery, and only wanted crews. I had only men enough for one gun's crew in the powder division. (The Charter Oak was valued at $15,000).

On the 8th of November we chased, captured and burned the bark D. Godfrey of Boston, bound for Valparaiso, with a cargo of excellent mess beef and pork. We regretted the destruction of this cargo, but the Shenandoah was full of provisions and room could not be found for more than twenty-two barrels of each kind. She was an old vessel and burned rapidly. Six of her men joined us and that made us number thirty-five men.

The D. Godfrey was a valuable prize. The following day was devoted to chasing and boarding foreign vessels. The engineers were engaged making iron plates for strengthening the deck in rear of guns, to which train tackles were to be hooked, as the deck was of soft pine and only four inches thick.

On the 10th of November we communicated with the Anna Jane, a Danish brig, and offered her master a chronometer, a barrel of beef and one of bread to relieve us of certain prisoners. He accepted our offer and we transferred the prisoners of our first and third captures to the protection of the Danish flag.

The chronometer given the Danish master was taken from the Alena.

# CHAPTER SIX

Soon after separating from the Danish brig we captured and scuttled the American brig Susan of New York, bound to the Rio Grande with coal. She was a long time out from Cardiff and we were disposed to think her master was not sorry to fall in with the Shenandoah.

Three of her crew joined us, which made our number thirty-eight. The prize was very old and very rickety. She leaked badly and got along at a snail's pace. Barnacles grew to her bottom and the crew was constantly employed at the pump in keeping the water down during calm weather or very light winds.

An ingenious plan had been devised before she left port to keep her afloat. To the pump was attached a shaft one half the beam of the vessel, and to the other end a wheel and buckets which resembled one side of a steamboat. The immersion of the buckets depended on her draft of water and the quantity of water discharged by the pump depended upon the velocity of the vessel through the water. Now what quantity of water per gallon was discharged per hour from the big Susan? That's a conundrum.

When she was first seen the steamboat side was exposed to our view and it was not until after a good scrutiny that her probable character was developed.

The sun was a few degrees above a brilliant western horizon and was sinking slowly to rest on the 11th instant when a sail was seen southwest of us on the port tack, standing to the southwest. I immediately gave chase, calculating that if the chase was equal in speed to the Shenandoah and allowing for errors of judgment in her distance we should be in hail of her soon after midnight. This was our first night chase, and few eyes were closed, so curious were we to know the character of the fair creature. Some doubted if we ever would see her again, while others thought the Shenandoah had entered on a dangerous speculation. Nothing is to be gained if risk is not taken.

A few minutes after midnight a ship was in full view. Her appearance was investigated through night glasses, while a boat was being prepared to communicate with her. Now that she was in hail, Lieutenant Whittle hailed her and asked her nationality. She proved to be the American clipper ship Kate Prince, with a neutral cargo of coal. She was ransomed on bond for $40,000.[29]

The boarding officer expressed regret it was necessary to ransom her, because all of her crew desired to join the Shenandoah and the captain's wife was a southern woman who desired the ship burned because she was not fast and she wished to sail in the Shenandoah.

Her crew numbered twenty-one seamen and would have been a great acquisition to our steamer. Late in the afternoon of the same day we chased and captured the American bark Adelaide Pendergrast of Baltimore, under Buenos Aires colors.

Her master, (Williams), could produce no bill of sale, and did not know of an absolute sale. She was ordered to

[29] Bonding or ransoming a vessel simply meant that a Confederate cruiser set a sum on a captured ship based on her total value and her cargo. This sum was to have been paid the Confederacy after the end of hostilities. Of course none of the shipowners honored such ransoms.

be prepared for firing and the order was partly executed, when an officer produced a letter for her consignee at Rio, which prevented her destruction.

She was sailing under false colors and her owner placed her master in a false position, neither informing him of the nationality of the vessel nor providing him with a bill of sale. She gave bond for $24,000. We had transferred our prisoners to the Kate Prince.

On the 13th of November, we chased, captured and burned the American schooner Lizzie M. Stacy of Boston, bound around the Cape of Good Hope for Honolulu, Island of Oahu on sale. She was new and fast. Her crew, three in all, joined the Shenandoah, which increased our number to 41.

This schooner would have made a capital cruiser, and I would gladly have fitted her out for the purpose, but for the scarcity of seamen. We could not spare ten of the crew. The 17th of November we crossed the line and old Neptune with his wife and barber, came on board and found most of his victims among the officers. Lieutenant Lee, always gay and happy, was the only officer who had crossed the line and he enjoyed arraigning his messmates before the court of the god of the sea, and participated in the preparations for their admission to his favor. Tar and soap for the barber's use and water from a donkey engine which threw a stream two inches in diameter over the unlucky victim is the ordeal through which each one passed upon his introduction to the line where Neptune is supposed to hold his court. The officer of the watch, Lieutenant Grimball, felt sure of escape in his position. I took charge of the deck and Grimball was carried off to his stateroom, where he prepared himself for his immersion and submitted with a good grace.

Our course now lay south along the coast of Brazil, and with a trade wind the ship boomed away splendidly. Nothing of interest occurred after crossing the equatorial line, except the exciting chase, the catching and boarding ships, until the 4th of December, when the American whale ship Edward, of and out of New Bedford, (three months) was captured. This capture took place in latitude 37 degrees 47 minutes south, fifty miles southeast of the Island of Tristan da Cunha, which was in sight. The Edward, (Captain North), had taken a right whale and her crew was engaged in "cutting out," i.e., cutting the fish and hoisting it on board.

The crew was so intensely occupied with the whale that the Shenandoah came within easy range unobserved. The fish is called right whale to distinguish it from the sperm and other whales. The outfit of the Edward was of excellent quality, and we lay by her two days, replenishing the Shenandoah with what we were in want of. We removed from her 100 barrels of beef and as many of pork, besides several thousand pounds of ship biscuit, the best we had ever eaten, put up in large whiskey seasoned hogsheads capable of holding 300 gallons of oil. We found also a quantity of whale line, cotton canvas, blocks, etc. Two of her boats were new and they were removed to the Shenandoah in place of her old and worthless ones. She was burned, and I visited a settlement on the northwest side of Tristan da Cunha and arranged with the chief man, (a Yankee) of the island who was called governor, to receive the crew of the Edward, most of whom were Sandwich Islanders (Kanakas). I furnished the governor with six weeks rations, which was considered sufficient, for the crew, as no doubt a vessel would touch there soon after my departure and would take them away. The governor's sympathies were altogether with the South, and like every other unprejudiced mind, considered the war Northern aggression, cruel and suicidal in the extreme. After remaining a few hours off the island of Tristan da Cunha I took my departure for Sydney, Australia, but gave the Shenandoah course for Cape Town, and so soon as much of the highland sank below the horizon, and the Island of Tristan da Cunha was blue in the distance, I steered a course south of east and soon struck those western gales which blow invariably south of 43 degrees with more or less violence. I have since heard that the Federal gunboat Dacotah, Commander Raymond Rodgers, took prisoners from the island on board the Dacotah and visited Cape Town, where he hoped to find the Shenandoah. The carpenter of the Edward joined us and was an excellent man. The crew now numbered 42. Whale ships are valuable when the cargo is oil, bone and furs. The Edward was not a valuable prize. ($20,000).

The register and papers of a whaling vessel resemble those of ordinary vessels in commerce. The strength of these vessels, many of which were built fifty years ago, prove the high estimate which American shipwrights then placed upon the power necessary to enable vessels to contend successfully against the storms of the ocean. The timber then used was double that now employed, and while greater strength was secured by the introduction of such large timbers, space for cargo was diminished. The improvements which the last thirty years have introduced in naval architecture have so revolutionized former theories that those old hulks have been turned over to whaling, and it was found to be a profitable trade until the Shenandoah got among them. These ships I fancy were built of the live-oak of New England. I believe the live-oak of Florida surpasses that of all other countries.

The whaling vessels vary from 90 to 100 feet in length with great beam, consequently they can be turned around more easily then vessels of greater length; powerful in construction, dull sailers, and sheathed for forty feet from the stern, which is generally shod with iron, they are calculated to resist contact with ice which floats in detached floes or pilot ice some sixteen feet in thickness and in an abundance in Bering Sea and northwards. They are equipped with boats much elevated at either end and strongly built. On the stempost are fitted collars for lines to pass over when attached to a whale. These lines are made of white hemp from 1½ to 2½ inches in circumference, varying from 100 to 250 fathoms (600 to 1500 feet) in length, and coiled in large tubs, (made to fit the boats expressly for this purpose) a precautionary measure to secure their easy flight and keep them from being entangled, which might cause the boat to capsize, so rapidly does the whale move when struck by a harpoon, the lance, and a two-inch muzzle blunderbuss, of short barrel, constructed of iron, and weighing about 40 pounds.

The projectile used is an elongated explosive shell of 12 inches in length. The blunderbuss is handled by a powerful and expert whalesman and discharged into the animal when near enough. The fuse is short, burns quickly, and explodes the shell causing instant death.

The whale floats to the surface of the water when the men attach a line to the head by sharp hooks, and tow the fish alongside the vessel when they proceed to cut it up.

A part of the midship section of the vessel is converted into a blubber room and into which the fish, after being cut up, is thrown. The boiling process for oil is proceeded with as quickly as possible. The arrangements for boiling the blubber are found on deck between the fore and main-mast, built of masonry and barred against accident in heavy weather. In the center of the masonry are one or more large cauldrons into which the blubber is placed, and after the oil is extracted, the refuse is used for making fire and produces an intense heat. The whalers carry hogs and this refuse is used for fattening them and they eat ravenously. The hogsheads used for receiving the oil vary in size from two to three hundred gallons. The greater part of these are shaken up when delivered to the vessels in port and put together upon the ship when wanted, consequently their stowage is closer.

Those hogsheads which have contained flour in bags, hams, cordage, clothing, ship biscuits, when emptied, are filled with oil. The odor from a whaling ship is horribly offensive, but it is not worse than that of the green hide vessels from South America, which can be smelt [sic] fifty miles in a favorable wind.

The bones of the whale are taken on board and placed in the bone room; from these the offensive exhalation is too horrible to relate. After our departure from Tristan da Cunha, the Shenandoah was put under canvas, and the propeller triced up.

While the engineer was securing the propeller he discovered a crack entirely across the brass band on the coupling of the propeller shaft. This was a serious matter and further examination satisfied him that the ship must have been in this condition when she came into the hands of the agent but the propeller being in the water, it was not examined.

It must have been known to her former owners before she was purchased and left the English dock. A temporary arrangement could be made to remedy this break but no comforting reliance was to be placed upon it, for the revolving of the shaft would most probably loosen the screw in the brass band, which, in their turn would grind away the lignum vital bearing and seriously injure the stern post.

Cape Town was the only place short of Melbourne at which such repairs could be made, and after considering the matter, I decided to cross the Indian Ocean, under sail, hoping for a continuance of the same good fortune which had accompanied us during the seven preceding weeks. The ship was given a more southerly course that she might sooner reach the strong west winds, which prevail in the belt which encircles the world south of the parallel of 40 degrees with more violence than in the corresponding belt north of the same parallel in north latitude. Such has been my experience.

We crossed the meridian of Greenwich on the 11th of December in a fresh west gale and a sea running high. The ship rolled very deep, owing to the large quantity of coal in her hold and steered a little wild owing to her being by the head, but all sharp and narrow vessels of great length have a tendency to roll deep, while this great length gives stability to a wind.

I was instructed to pass the meridian of the Cape of Good Hope by the first of January, 1865, and at noon of the 17th of December, the Shenandoah was east of that meridian, with a west wind following fast. The speed of the ship varied with the strength of the wind.

Upon reaching the parallel of 43 degrees 30 minutes south the wind was a revolving gale, the path of which lay southeast freshening with increasing violence. It became

117

evident that to continue the course would be hazardous, and by changing the course to the north of east the ship would make better weather in a short time. She rolled so heavily that sea after sea tumbled in over her railing and her preparations for freeing herself were so indifferent that water was several inches deep, flooding all the apartments on that deck.

A Christmas dinner had been prepared of the captured supplies, but it was quite impossible to sit long enough to enjoy it, except under difficulties. Most of the dishes left the table for the deck, and notwithstanding the disappointment at the loss of a good dinner, there was still life enough among us left to record it as an incident in the sailor's life. Should I ever again make a trip to Australia, I would go very little south of the howling forties. The ship ran out of the gale and found a more genial clime north of the parallel of 40.

The squalls of snow and hail during that gale were frightful. On the 29th of December, the wind moderated as rapidly as it had risen, and was then nearly at south, bringing along with it an occasional squall of fine rain, and leaving an ugly cross sea that seemed undecided how and where to expend itself. It broke against the sides of the Shenandoah, sending fine spray through the open seams of the hull into the berth deck.

The decks were then leaking dreadfully, and the bedding was more or less wet. A wet watch is uncomfortable enough, but to nod in a chair or be forced to turn into a wet bed is even worse, as we found. While the ship wallowed in that broken sea under short canvas, a sail was seen from aloft astern of us, and could be seen from the deck through the fine squalls of rain. It was soon known what sail she was under, and the Shenandoah was made to hold her luff to prevent the stranger passing to windward of her.

Every glass watched eagerly the unsuspecting "critter," whose hull was painted white and green, and looked like game for the sportsmen. On inquiring her nationality she hoisted a flag which was so faded we found it difficult to recognize, but on approaching us it was what we were directed to search for.

She continued to approach us and raised a blackboard on which was written her position at noon. Finding she could not pass to windward of the Shenandoah, she kept away and ran close to her stern when our flag was hoisted, and "bang" went a gun.

This brought her by the wind quickly, and an officer was despatched in a boat to communicate with her and to send her master to the Shenandoah with the papers. She was the American bark Delphine of Bangor, bound for Akyab for a load of rice intended for the Federal armies. When Nichols was informed that his vessel was a prize and would be destroyed, he replied, "it may cause the death of my wife to remove her. The report of the gun has made her very ill."

He was referred to the surgeon upon whose report I should be concerned. The surgeon visited the lady and reported to me that there would be no risk in removing her to the Shenandoah, and a chair was prepared, a whip fitted to the main yard, and very soon two women and a child were safely landed on our deck.

When in the act of leaving my cabin, into which they were invited, Mrs. Nichols asked in a stentorian voice if I was captain, what I intended to do with them, and where would they be landed.

119

"On St. Paul,[30] madam, if you like."

"Oh, no, never. I would rather remain with you."

I was surprised to see in the sick lady a tall, finely proportioned woman of twenty-six years, in robust health, evidently possessing a will and a voice of her own.

We took only the livestock from the Delphine and burned her. This capture increased the crew of the Shenandoah to forty-seven, several of whom were Germans for whom we felt little sympathy. The Delphine had on board machinery for cleaning rice and it was stated to be the property of a Frenchman. She was put before the wind in flames, but did not run far before her sails were consumed, and her masts fell, one after the other, over her sides.

Thus closed the thirty-first day of December, the last day of the year, amid fire, smoke and ruin, and the fourth year since the Civil War began. How many of our dear friends and companions had in that time gone to that undiscovered country from whose bourne no traveller returns. Full of hope in the commencement as we then were, how many had seen the light of hope go out with their lives, their dying eyes fixed upon a struggling country, upon desolated homes, broken family ties, and all lost that makes life enjoyable. Such thoughts gave me food for reflection.

[30] St. Paul Island.

# CHAPTER SEVEN

The first of January, 1865, was a frisky day. The sea was smooth and a fair wind wafted us along. The new year was welcomed by the hoisting of a flag which had never before been unfurled to the breeze. The Shenandoah had now been in commission two months and eleven days, and had destroyed or ransomed more property than her cost.

I believe the case is without parallel in naval history. The prisoners had become quite accustomed to their situation and no longer entertained a doubt as to their personal safety. The master of the Delphine expressed shame for having attempted to save his ship by pretending that his wife was ill, and said,

"I didn't think a lie wrong under the circumstances."

On the following day we saw the Islands of Amsterdam and St. Paul and stopped at the latter to explore in search of American whalers. An armed boat was sent in charge of Lieutenant Grimball with orders to destroy all property found on the island belonging to citizens of the United States.

After a close search the boat returned and Grimball reported having seen two Frenchmen who had been left on the island from a French whale ship, to catch and salt fish, while she visited the Island of Amsterdam.

Two small patches of cultivated ground and a few shanties were all he saw. The crater of an extinct volcano forms the little Bay of St. Paul, which was alive with a variety of fish good to eat. The boat could barely pass the reef from its shallowness, and the fish could have been taken from the water by hand.

The margin of the crater was gradually consumed and weakened until near the surface of the water, when an east gale broke away its caps and the sea rolled in, forming the Bay of St. Paul.

The officers brought fish, eggs, a few chickens, and a penguin from the settlement. The penguin was not so large as some I have seen, but in every respect of the same species as those found at the Falkland Islands. Their note is identical with the bray of that unmentionable animal. They are covered with gray down, are unable to fly, and walk with military erectness.

Someone pinned around the neck of our penguin a rag resembling a shawl in its folds, which created much merriment, and as the bird walked away Mrs. Nichols exclaimed,

"For all the world like an old woman."

This lady had somewhat softened in tone, and we admired her for the discipline she observed toward Mr. Nichols.

The ship was under steam off the island, and after taking our departure, sail was made and the propeller was triced up. The band of the propeller coupling was broken again and an additional number of screws were entered to secure it. A course was then given for Cape Leeuwin and the Shenandoah, on the 23rd of January, met an east wind, most unfavorable for us, and with it came a westerly current, driving the ship away from her course, and working to windward was no easy task under the circumstances for even so smart a craft as the Shenandoah.

It was absolutely necessary that the ship should be docked

122

and, notwithstanding the injury which was already done or might be done to the bearings by using the propeller, I felt obliged to use steam, because the vessel must be docked at Melbourne, and I desired to reach there in time to communicate with the mail steamer which would leave that port on the 26th of January, and if we missed her we would not have another opportunity to send letters to England for some time.

Cape Otway was made on the morning of the 25th instant, and soon after the Heads to Port Phillip were visible. A pilot boat came to us and we received a pilot, who inquired why we wished the ship taken into Hobson's Bay. Before I could reply he said, "My orders are peremptory about Confederate vessels."

I gave a satisfactory reply to his instructions and the steamer was pointed for the entrance to the port. The Shenandoah was visited at the Heads by a health officer who communicated by telegram to Melbourne the character of the Shenandoah, and a little before sunset she dropped her anchors in Hobson's Bay, cheered from densely crowded steamboats.

Newspapers were pitched on board. Cheer after cheer greeted us from the generous, brave hearted Englishmen and Australians, who believed in the justice of our cause. We were prepared for the reception. The pilot had said, "You have a great many friends in Melbourne."[31]

Lieutenant Grimball was sent with the following communication, addressed to

[31] There was also a strong pro-northern feeling in Australia. Petty Officer Hunt tells of one party that ended in a free-for-all because some northern sympathizer had made a remark. Like a large segment of the people of Great Britain, the Australians hated slavery.

His Excellency Sir Charles Darling, K. C. B.,
   Captain General, Governor in Chief, and
      Vice-Admiral, Melbourne, Australia:
Sir:

I have the honor to announce to your Excellency the arrival of the Confederates States steamer Shenandoah, under my command, in Port Phillip, this afternoon, and I have also to communicate that the steamer's machinery requires repairs, and that I am in want of coals. I desire your Excellency to grant permission for me to make the necessary repairs, to take in a [load] of coals, to enable me to get to sea as quickly as possible. I desire also your Excellency's permission to land my prisoners. I shall observe the neutrality.

I have the honor to be your obedient servant,
                                        James I. Waddell.


On the following morning, soon after daylight, the prisoners deserted, taking all their luggage with them much to my comfort. I received the following reply to my letter of the 25th:[32]

(Letter No. 34.)


(Letter No. 35.)


Custom House, Melbourne, 30 January, 1865.
Sir:

I am directed by his Excellency the Governor to acknowledge the receipt of your letter of the 28th instant, and of your memorandum of this day's date, inclosed in a letter addressed to you by Messrs. Langland Brothers and Company, a copy of which letter, with your subjoined memorandum is returned herewith, and to inform you it will be necessary that a list of

[32] Letter No. 34 which Waddell refers to is missing. Apparently he sent an answer on the twenty-eighth, which in turn was answered by the Governor's secretary on the thirtieth.

124

the supplies required for the immediate use of your vessel, together with one of the prisoners, et cetera, as I suggested in my previous communication, should be sent in for the guidance of his Excellency, before five o'clock on the 31st instant. I have it further in command to inform you that his Excellency has appointed a board consisting of Mr. Payne, Inspector and Secretary of the Steam Navigation Board; Mr. Elder, Superintendent of the Marine Yard at this place, and Mr. Wilson, Government Marine Engineer, to go on board the Shenandoah, and to examine and report whether the vessel is now in a fit state to proceed to sea, or what repairs are necessary.

I have the honor to be, sir, your obedient servant,

James C. Francis.

J. I. Waddell, Esqu.,
Lieutenant-Commanding C. S. Steamer Shenandoah.

Confederate States Steamer Shenandoah<br>January 30, 1865.

To the Honorable Commissioner of Trade and Customs:
Sir:

In reply to your communication of this day's date, I have to state, the immediate supplies required for the officers and crew under my command consists of fresh meat, vegetables, and bread daily, and that the sea supplies required will be brandy, rum, champagne, port, sherry, beer, porter, molasses, lime juice and light material for summer wear for my men, etc. In regard to a list of prisoners, I have to communicate that all those persons whom, on the high seas, I considered my prisoners (and of whom I wrote to his Excellency the Governor) left the ship without my knowledge, in shore boats, soon after my arrival in this port. In regard to the board which his Excellency the Governor has constituted for the examination of the Shenandoah, under my command, every facility will be extended to them.

I remain, very respectfully, sir,<br>James I. Waddell,<br>Lieutenant Commanding.

Port Phillip Foundry,
Melbourne, 30 January, 1865.

Captain Waddell,
Confederate Steamer of War Shenandoah:
Sir:

At your request we beg to report that it will be absolutely necessary to put the Shenandoah on the Government slip, as after inspection by the diver, he reports that the lining of the outer sternback is entirely gone and will have to be replaced. As to the time required, as three days will elapse before she is slipped, we will not be able to accomplish the repairs within ten days from date.

Yours, etc.,
Langlands Brothers & Co.

Respectfully submitted to the Honorable Commissioner of Trade and Customs, with the request that it may be returned.

James I. Waddell,
Lieutenant Commanding, C.S.N.

Several of our crew having been induced to desert the steamer through the influence of the American consul and his emissaries, I addressed a note to the chief of police on the subject.[33]

Having received several anonymous letters concerning a threatened destruction of the Shenandoah while in port, by emissaries of the American consul, I considered it a prudent precaution to address a note to Captain Lyttleton, Superintendent of the Water Police, upon the subject. Subjoined is Captain Lyttleton's reply.

Police Department, Superintendent's Office
Melbourne, February 8, 1865.

Sir:

I have the honor to acknowledge the receipt of your letter of the 31st ultimo, requesting police protection for the Con-

[33] Neither Hunt nor the United States Consul makes mention of any desertions of the Shenandoah's crew.

126

federate war steamer Shenandoah. I beg to inform you that I have instructed the Williamstown and water police to give particular attention to the vessel. I should have replied to your letter before, but that from some cause which I shall inquire into, it only reached me on the morning of the 4th instant.

I have the honor to be, sir, your most obedient servant,

Thomas  Lyttleton,
Superintendent.

Captain Waddell,
Confederate War Steamer Shenandoah.

There was a Mr. MacFarlin, a customs official, who did not have sufficient intelligence to recognize the distinction between a national and piratical vessel, who for many days kept watch over the Shenandoah with his assistants, under disguise of friendly visits to her officers.

I took occasion to inform him of the indelicacy of those visits, and explained to him the difference between a privateer, a piratical, a merchant, and a national vessel and we were not troubled by him quite so much as before.

A considerable degree of excitement prevailed on Thursday, the 26th day of January, 1865, when it became known in Melbourne, Australia, that an interesting visitor had anchored not far from the Sandridge Railway pier in Hobson's Bay. A sensation was created by the arrival of the Shenandoah that had not been caused by the comet, although many believed that the long tailed one would run foul of the fifth continent before making off for some other part of the world.

Several of the officers of the Shenandoah visited the city and, as was to be expected, excited much eager attention. Apparently as a kind of protest against the recognition of the stranger, those American houses whose sympathies were known to be strongly Federal hoisted the Stars and Stripes, but there was no similar demonstration on the part of the firms whose affections were believed to be the other way. This, I believe, was owing to an impression that the exhibition of the Confederate flag would be protested against by the American consul. A very strong feeling was more than once manifested by some of the citizens, and in one instance a knock-down between partisans was with difficulty prevented.

When it was known publicly that the executive counsel had no objection to the presence of the Shenandoah for a limited period in the neighborhood of the bay defences, invisible as they were to the common eye, the quidnuncs of Melbourne rushed en masse on the water in yachts, steamers and small boats. The officers of the ship were not only courteous but assertive, and by their personal presence and pertinent seamanlike remarks, furnished the opportunity of getting on board and viewing the ship without pushing and cramming. Not that there was much to see except a neat merchant ship with a telescopic funnel, a lot of machinery somewhere, some big, ugly guns, and a couple of little ones, for a wonder stamped with a crown.

The ensign was admired, and the pattern should not be forgotten. It had thirteen stars, emblazoned white upon blue transversely in a field of red, the fly of the flag being white. The stars and stripes were hoisted over many places of business in the city constantly, of course in compliment to the Confederate cruiser.

The enemy's gallantry was not expected to go further. I would be sorry, knowing our northern friends as well as I do, to believe that the hoisting of the stars and stripes was done either out of defiance or disrespect. Burn, sin, and destroy was the watchword of the Shenandoah.

That the orders were strictly obeyed, the best evidence exists in the Alabama Claims Court. The pestilential scouring of the seas is repulsive to all civilized men. Had the Confederates a mercantile marine, it would have been served with no less severity. We know the fate of such blockade runners as were seized, and may therefore entertain a very decided opinion as regards the destination of a large fleet of merchant ships unfortunate enough to fall in the way of any Federal man-of-war.

Virtuous indignation from American sources were poured upon the ministry, which allowed the Shenandoah to refit, take in coals, and generally put herself in a sea-going condition. This was to be expected, seeing how high feeling runs even now between fathers, sons and brothers.

It has embittered not for one generation alone all the feelings that were once so pleasant, fraternal and agreeable, but an abiding hatred has been engendered between those who years gone by would have laid down their lives for each other's protection.

As between nation and nation at war, when the bugle sings truce, the soldiers cross the lines, smoke and chat and drink together, it is devoutly prayed that the people of this, our common country, will relegate to their kind the few pestilential politicians who still insist on the bloody shirt.

The doors of the Melbourne Club were hospitably opened to the officers of the Shenandoah. They were royally entertained and received by a society composed to a considerable extent, of government officials, including judges of the courts.

The entertainment was a courtesy which the club always

extends to strangers, and the presence of the company was an expression of sympathy for a gallant people engaged in resisting a wicked aggression. Although there was a general sympathy in the community for the Confederate cause as kindly exhibited in many ways in the hospitalities shown to the officers of the Shenandoah, it was equally true there were sympathies warmly disposed toward the Federals.

The reception and shelter granted to the Shenandoah had given serious offense to this party, and the abortive efforts to discredit the character of the officers and crew of the ship in connection with the cause for which they were in arms had, as was openly asserted, been followed by the still more unworthy course of tampering with the allegiance of the crew.

The ship had been taken on the slip for repairs, fourteen of her crew had been induced to desert, and when a formal representation of the matter was made to the chief commissioner of police and a request made for their apprehension and arrest, it was declared beyond his province to interfere.

Do you believe a similar request from a Federal commander would have been declared beyond his province to interfere? It was charged by the American consul that the commander had violated the British Foreign Enlistment Act and the hospitalities shown to him, by the enrollment of men for the service in which he was engaged.

I had offers of service of all kinds, in every department of duty, including nurses to tend the sick and wounded. In fact, I could not walk the streets of Melbourne without being waylaid with eager candidates, agents of the American consul, for employment.

One particular instance may be cited of enthusiasm for the cause, and of my scrupulous regard for the duties im-

130

posed by the laws of neutrality and hospitality. An elderly woman with a lad came alongside the ship. The woman urgently besought me to take the lad and, in hope of gaining her desire, exhibited papers to show that the lad was born in Mobile, Alabama, and only asked to serve in the cause of his country.

As I have stated elsewhere, the vessel was, by permission of the colonial authorities, placed on the government slip for repairs. Those repairs were near completion, and I had directed that she be launched at high water on the following day.

Intense excitement was created in the public mind when it became known that the colonial authorities had seized the Shenandoah. The whole matter, partaking as it did of elements of interest quite unknown to any of us or the good people of Melbourne, was naturally made most of, and public conversation ran on few other topics.

The Monday previous, I was on shore, and Lieutenant Grimball was in charge of the Shenandoah. Superintendent Lyttleton and Inspector Beam of the Victorian police, with a magistrate's warrant to search for a person who was said to be a British subject, came on board. The cause of their visit was induced by deserters who had been employed by the American consul to give information that one Charlie, an Englishman, had shipped in the Shenandoah.[34]

No names could be given, but eventually a deserter named Madden swore that he could identify a person named Charlie as one who had been cook's assistant. On this information, which was sworn to, a search warrant was issued, and this the police officer named endeavored to inforce.

[34] This was "Charley the Cook" mentioned by the United States Consul in his dispatches.

Lieutenant Grimball refused to allow the search. After my return to the vessel the police officers came again, and I refused the search, and stated I had neither enlisted nor shipped any person for service in the Confederate cause since my arrival.

It is worthy of notice that an attempt was made to distort this statement into a similar pledge that the man or men were not on board, though it is well understood that there are stowaways who have their friends among a crew. As it was a part of the information given by the deserters that the new men wore the Confederate uniform, I gave the assurance that could hardly be so, because there were no such uniforms provided.

The narrative may be stayed here, to give a few reasons why I refused the search. First, the well known doctrine that a vessel of war is part of the territory of the country to which she belongs. Thus, reasoning from analogy, a British ship of war would not permit the civil authorities of a foreign port to search her, and in the well known case of Franz Müller, the murderer of Mr. Briggs, so closely was this practice adhered to, that the British constables were not allowed to effect the arrest, which was done by American policemen.

Having abided strictly by the terms of neutrality imposed during my visit, I asserted that the privileges of a vessel of war should remain intact. I was ready to offer the same assistance which an English vessel of war in a foreign port would render.

I was willing to order the police of the Shenandoah, viz., the master-at-arms and his posse, to make the search.

In fact, my offer was, in effect, to execute the warrant with the ship's police. The foreign police officers did not accept my offer, but I left the ship. The master-at-arms and his posse were ordered to make a more careful search of the vessel in addition to that which took place daily.

I sent two lieutenants and the master-at-arms to make a closer search. The lieutenants reported to me they had looked throughout the vessel and found no strangers. They had examined even the coal bunker. It was now about sundown. Long before that time I was aware of the presence of a large body of police bearing arms, who excluded all workmen from the yard, and in fact took possession of the government slip, on the cradle of which the Shenandoah was securely fixed.

Later a letter arrived, signed J. G. Francis, Chief Commissioner of Customs, inquiring, by direction of his Excellency the Governor, if execution of the warrant had been received and stating that till an answer was received, the facilities hitherto afforded to the Shenandoah would be suspended, id est, that work would cease on the Shenandoah.

I replied at once. The effect of my answer was to assert, first, that it was not consistent with British law to accept the contrary of a citation of facts and act thereupon. I was appealed to to reconsider my determination, but I informed his Excellency that execution of the warrant had not been refused, as no such person as the one specified was known to be on board, but permission to search the ship had been refused as such proceeding would be contrary to the dignity of the Confederate flag.

The services of the police of the ship had been offered, the shipping articles had been exhibited to the superintendent of police, and a search under the supervision of two lieutenants instituted, but no person found who had not shipped before the vessel entered Victorian waters.

I informed his Excellency, as commander of the Shenandoah, a representative of the Confederate Government in British waters, that no person was on board except those who belonged to the crew; that no one had been enlisted by any officer since my arrival, and that in no way had the neutrality of the port been violated.

I therefore, in the name of the Confederate States Government, entered my solemn protest against any obstruction that might cause my detention in that port. I had provided against attack, and disposed my small force as to secure the vessel against boarding. Of course, if an attack was made, the attacking party would have knocked away the props, and the vessel would have fallen from the slip and been rendered a hopeless ruin.

Some fifty men of the royal artillery were sent to the railroad station to start for the scene of action. An officer came to the men on duty at the Williamstown battery, but as high ground intervened, the guns were of no use, as they did not command the Government slip, nor were the guns at the pier put in use, which commanded that spot, why, I never learned.

Stories were told to the effect that one of the Government gun rafts was moved near to over awe any possible demonstration of strength by the Shenandoah. Why, the vessel lay on the slip as helpless as the Victorian Government could possibly desire. In the full belief that the ship would not be detained, I gave orders for her launch, and the tug Black Eagle was engaged for the purpose of being in readiness and near to. The manager of the slip explained he could not launch the ship, that he acted by order of the Government; whereupon, I stated in a communication to the Government that a refusal to permit the launch of the ship amounted to her seizure, and I respectfully begged to be informed if such was known to his Excellency the Governor and met with his approval.

This missive was taken on shore to the governor by Lieutenant Grimball, who was ordered not to return without an answer. The course which I proposed to pursue in case his Excellency was aware of the seizure, was to regard officers and men as prisoners of the British Government, to haul down the flag, and proceed with my command to London by the next mail boat.

The denouement was, that in answer to my request to know if his Excellency was aware that his act amounted to a seizure, permission [was given] to launch the Shenandoah. The following proclamation was published in the course of the afternoon:

> The suspension of the permission given to her Majesty's subjects to aid in the necessary repairs and supplies of the ship Shenandoah, dated the 14th instant, is relieved, in so far as launching the said vessel is concerned, which may be proceeded with accordingly.
>
> C. H. Darling, Governor, etc.

Steam was immediately ordered, and the vessel was launched about two hours after high water and taken into the stream, where she dropped a single anchor. I then informed the commissioner of trade and customs the Shenandoah could now take care of herself.

It will not be forgotten that the commissioner of trade and customs, who was a business partner of the American consul, and also a member of Governor Sir C. H. Darling's ministry, bore a conspicuous and ungenerous hostility to the Shenandoah's mission. Steam was kept up, the vessel lay at single anchor, and preparations were made for an early start the following day.

The ridicule and contempt which ever attach to ignorance, rashness and rudeness in high places, was never more conspicuous than by the British authorities in that portion of their empire. The obstructive and menacing attitude of the ministry towards the Shenandoah, while she lay hopeless on the slip at Williamstown, was publicly known. The movement, in my opinion, did not actually amount to a seizure, but it was something more than a close surveillance, for it interfered with the workmen who were engaged on repairs of the vessel with a view to her being made ready for sea.

It was an interposition of authority that ought never to have been made without there being full and well sustained grounds to call for it, and even then there should have been first ascertained if it were conformable to the law of nations to make such an offensive interference with the freedom of action of a foreign ship of war that was an unsuspecting participator of hospitality at the moment.

The question which first naturally arose on the case was, what cause, grave enough and sufficient of itself, had the ministry for the course they so hastily adopted and so soon afterwards abandoned, in reference to the Shenandoah? And next, assuming that they had what appeared to themselves sufficient cause, were they justified in attempting to coerce a foreign ship-of-war into what they regarded as proper conduct, by means similar to what they would employ against their own fellow subjects?

In neither case can I think an answer could be given that would acquit the ministry of gross ignorance of their duties, and also of rashness in giving effect to their ignorance, in supposing that they had possessed themselves of plausible

136

information of the Shenandoah's officers having enlisted men for the vessel contrary to the British Foreign Enlistment Act, they had not the right to attempt to compel the officers or crew to supply the means of converting that information into actual proof.

The Shenandoah's people were not the custodians of British law and least of all of a British law which ran counter to their own immediate interests as the British Foreign Enlistment Act did. The British authorities are the proper custodians of British law; with them alone it rests to take care that no breach of neutrality does take place in the event of an armed vessel of a belligerent power entering their ports and harbors. Suppose then they were informed on what they regarded as reliable information that the Shenandoah had shipped some colonial recruits, it would be only proof against the ministry that they had not so maintained the operation of the law of neutrality as to save it from violation. But it formed no ground for forcibly insisting upon the foreign ship, against which the breach of neutrality was alleged, to supplement their defective evidence in completing a charge against the ship itself.

The law of nations, as laid down by every authority, justifies foreigners in refusing their aid to carry out laws which are repugnant to their own interest. The Shenandoah's people could not therefore be intelligently called upon by the colonial authorities to lend their aid in proving that there were colonial recruits for the Confederate service stowed away on board their ship.

I was therefore justified in refusing to submit to the humiliation of a search. On the other hand, the dignified course for the authorities was not to act upon suspicion or meagre and incomplete information, or in any case to take half measures: but cause for inquiry having been shown, they were bound to investigate the matter from their own resources as thoroughly as possible, and if they became convinced of having obtained tangible and adequate proof of a breach of neutrality, then to proceed, if necessary, to extremities on their own peril and responsibility to vindicate the violated law of their country. But if their investigation did not eventuate in arming them with clear and positive proof of the violation of their law, then their course was to let the matter rest, and make no move whatever in it.

A power, acknowledged as a belligerent, even though it may not have yet established its separate independence, is, for all the purposes of the war of separation a de facto, distinct individual power. A ship of war belonging to such a power is recognized in the law of nations as a part of the territory of the power to which it belongs.

The foreign deck and the foreign territory are both alike inviolable by alien authorities, even in search of murderers, unless an extradition treaty exists between the governments of the respective powers concerned, under which treaty it is arranged that criminals are to be mutually given up.

# CHAPTER EIGHT

We felt no anxiety about Federal cruisers, for we foresaw that they would in all probability be as unsuccessful in finding the Shenandoah as they had been in their search for the Alabama. Sunday morning, the 19th day of February, saw the anchors of the Shenandoah on her bows, and at 8 o'clock she steamed from the anchorage toward the Heads of Port Phillip, a distance of thirty miles.

The pilot, Mr. Johnson, who had brought the Shenandoah in from sea, had since been so unfortunate as to run a vessel on a shoal, which had injured him in the opinions of many shipmasters. A brother of his called and stated the facts connected with his case, adding, "If you will let him take your steamer out he will be again on his feet."

His services were accepted, and he took the Shenandoah safely out. Soon we were on the bright blue sea, standing away from the land to the westward. The pilot left us with his farewell and good wishes, but it was not like the farewell we exchange with friends who from the ship's side, return to our own dear native shore with letters and last words of affectionate greeting to those we leave behind.

Impatiently we hurried our stranger pilot over the side, and no one said God speed. The vessels in sight were steering for Port Phillip where on their arrival would be reported our communication with them, and the direction taken by the Shenandoah. Soon after night the steamer's head was turned eastward toward Round Island in Bass Strait. Tas-

139

mania is the land south, no doubt was at one time a peninsula of Australia, and the islands in Bass Straits fragments.

The moon, with its soft sheen light, the clear atmosphere,
the frosty air, and the sky seemed more distant than I had
ever seen it before, and

> "The stars that over sprinkle
> All the heavens, seemed to twinkle
> With a crystalline delight." E. A. P.

At sunrise the Shenandoah had fairly entered Bass Strait
with the wind at N. E. light and good for steaming. The
steamer was continued under steam until Cape Howe bore
per compass N. N. W., when sail was made and the propeller
hoisted up. The ship's company was now increased.

We had received thirty-four young American seamen and
eight others of different nationalities in exchange for our
Irish Americans, sixteen Germans and a Negro, who had
deserted in Hobson's Bay, under a promise of $100 cash from
the American consul.

This increase placed on the deck seventy-two men of
different ratings, all adventurous and accustomed to a hard
life. The first lieutenant, Mr. Whittle, now saw a force under
his direction nearly sufficient to keep the Shenandoah in
good condition. These men had smuggled themselves on
board the steamer the night before we left Hobson's Bay. A
sergeant, a corporal and three privates formed the nucleus
for a marine guard, and their uniforms were immediately
ordered.

We were supplied with a tailor. The sergeant, Geo. P.
Canning, represented himself to have been aide-de-camp to
Lieutenant-General Leonidas Polk, formerly Bishop Polk,
and the wound which resulted in his death, some months

140

after, he declared to have received in the Battle of Shiloh.

There were several representations from New England among the crew. Where is it we do not find that irrepressible people? To find them on the deck of a Confederate cruiser taking delight in the destruction of the property of their countrymen, was indeed extraordinary. Perhaps not more so than the awful spectacle of a facsimile in a Southern-born man.

There are a multiplicity of reasons for that war among politicians, those who wore the bloody shirt and keep clear of gunpowder, and it is a pity that unoffending citizens should lay down their all for those who made the trouble and were not the ones to fight, but the dirty thing is over and we should feel privileged to live under the flag and be content. In no civilized country have the people been so ruthlessly oppressed and so cruelly despoiled as were the Southern people during the long period of Republican rule. No man tries to apologize for the wrongs inflicted on a helpless people, at whose throats federal bayonets were pressed to terrify them, while scoundrels of every profession from other states rioted and gloated over them.

The members of a proud family would avoid thinking or speaking of an ancestor who was hung for murder or a brother who was lynched for horse stealing, so all good citizens like to ignore the events to which I have referred.

To the north of us lay the Middleton, Lord Howe, and Norfolk Islands. They are contiguous to the coast of Australia and are in easy communication with Sydney. Our long delay at Melbourne gave the American consul ample time to warn American shipping of the danger to which it was exposed.

If the ship had been favored with a good wind, I should

have visited the whaling ground of each of those islands, but it was very certain the birds had taken shelter, and I would probably find them further north. The delay of the Shenandoah had operated against us in the South Pacific.

The whaling fleet of that ocean had received warning and had either suspended its fishing in that region or had taken shelter in the neighboring ports. The presence of the Shenandoah in the South Pacific dispersed the whaling fleet of that sea, though no captures were made there. The wind held on N. E. until the ship had nearly reached the meridian of the Three Kings, which is west of the most northwesterly point of North New Zealand. Now a favorable wind blew and the Shenandoah was steered north, passing between Fearn and Conway Islands, thence along the Figi, Rotumah and Ellen Islands.[35] These islands being within the tropics are covered with verdure and luxuriant undergrowth, the temperature of the air varying with the strength of the breeze.

When north of Fearn Island, a revolving gale from northeast came on. I had no choice as to which tack to lay the Shenandoah on, for there were too many islands west of her whose exact locality was inaccurately determined, to risk her on the starboard tack, nor could she be run for the same reason. Fortunately the gale worked westward, and the steamer was kept out of the path.

In twenty-three years of service I had never seen such a succession of violent squalls. The vessel was enveloped in salt mist and knocked by every angry sea. The machinery acted all right, and the ship's preparations for contending with adverse weather were so complete that wind and wave seemed now bent upon her destruction.

35 Fiji, Rotuma, Ellice Islands.

142

I have never seen a vessel in a gale stand up better to it or receive less water on deck. Her easy motion and steadiness throughout that gale increased our admiration of her.

The gale lasted four days and a calm followed. On the 21st of March, in latitude 8°35′ south and longitude 172°37′ east, failing to pick up the trade wind, and being wearied from excessive heat and a deluge of rain, I ordered steam and steered in a north direction in search of the trades, sighted Drummond Island, and ran sufficiently near to communicate with natives who came out in their canoes.

The native islanders are of copper color, short in stature, athletic in form, intelligent and docile; were without a rag of clothing. A day or two after leaving Drummond Island we communicated with a schooner from Honolulu on a trading voyage among the islands in search of tortoise shell, and from her I obtained some valuable information. Ship under sail again with a fine trade wind, came in near view of Strong Island and, putting the vessel under steam, we ran near enough to take a view of the harbor of Chabrol, which is a place of rendezvous for whale ships.

The harbor was empty. I skirted all sides of the island but the north side. I ordered the propeller to be lifted, and made sail for the island of Punipet[36] or Ascension, one of the Caroline Group.

The Shenandoah now had a fine trade wind and was running smoothly and rapidly along toward the island, which came in view during the forenoon of the day following our visit to Strong Island.

A little before midday the Shenandoah had approached sufficiently near to distinguish five sail at anchor close in with the land, and we began to think if they were not whale

[36] Ponape.

ships it would be a very good April fool. The Honolulu schooner was the only sail we had seen from the 20th of February to April 1st, which was evidence that the South Pacific whaling fleet had taken flight. We were never on any occasion so long without seeing a sail, and sailing over almost unknown and strange seas produced a dullness and monotony intolerable.

The ship was steaming along the land when a small boat came in sight with a single sitter. He was an Englishman and a pilot to the Lea Harbor in which the five vessels were at anchor. He was an escaped convict, many years from Sydney, Australia, to the Island of Ascension, and married a native woman.

He was questioned about the vessels and the safety of the port for anchorage. The harbor was most too confining for a vessel of the Shenandoah's length, and there were a few known dangers below the surface of the water. The pilot was directed to anchor the Shenandoah inside a long reef which extends almost across the entrance to the harbor, rendering the approach very narrow. The flag was not yet shown and the pilot was in ignorance of our nationality, nor did he ask any questions.

The preparations for anchoring being made, I accompanied the pilot and kept with him until the steamer was anchored. Three of the vessels in port hoisted the American flag. The fourth hoisted the flag of Oahu.

There is in that snug little harbor about mid channel a rock awash and the Shenandoah was near to it, but unavoidably so. It was necessary to secure her from swinging and to provide against accident hawsers were run out from her quarters to stout trees, and her bow anchors being down she was tied up. Four armed boats were then des-

144

patched with orders to capture the vessels and to send their officers, ship papers, log books, charts and instruments for navigation to the Shenandoah, and the officers were directed to remain in charge of their respective prizes until further orders.

These boats were the second and third cutters and two whale boats, respectively in charge of Lieutenants Grimball, Chew, Lee and Scales. These boats varied in dimensions, neither of them being over 32 or under 28 feet in length, and having less than six feet beam. They were strongly built and carried water and provisions for thirty persons for twenty days, oars, sails, masts, compass, lanterns, slow match, hatchet and a small chest for pistols and cutlasses.

Seven men constituted a prize crew for any duty. Each lieutenant had one or more subordinate officers, each had his special duty assigned him independent of the other. The charts captured were all important, because the Shenandoah was not furnished with such charts as whalers use, which show every track they make where they have been most successful in taking whales.

With such charts in my possession, I not only held a key to the navigation of all the Pacific Islands, the Okhotsk and Bering Seas, and the Arctic Ocean, but the most probable localities for finding the great Arctic whaling fleet of New England, without a tiresome search.

After the boats had left the steamer the flag was hoisted to the spanker gaff and a gun was fired. This signal, announcing the character of the Shenandoah, aroused all the surrounding country. The natives along the bay shore who were gazing at the vessel sought shelter in the bushes, and the American whalers hauled down their flags.

Some officer, directing the pilot's attention to our flag,

asked him if he knew it. He replied he had never before seen it, but as the boats were gone after the Yankees, it might be Jeff Davis's flag, for he had heard of a big war in America, and that in all the big battles the South had whipped the Yankees.

When I told him what we were, he said, "Well, well, I never thought I would live to see Jeff Davis's flag."

The popular abbreviation of ex-President Jefferson Davis's name was as common in Ascension as elsewhere. With the natives it bore the signification of king, and they were made familiar with the abbreviation through the mouths of whale-men who visit that port to purchase yamas and fruits pre-paratory to their leaving for fishing north and as far as the Atlantic Ocean.

The pilot told me there were five tribes on the island, each having a king and nobility. The cocoanut was the cur-rency, and metal money had no value with them except as an ornament. They are fond of finery, like tobacco and liquor, and are glad to get powder and shot. No principle of honor controls them in their intercourse, but fear of injury makes them respect whatever compact they solemnly enter upon.

Is not that very much the case with white people? It strikes me the white tribe has more educated scoundrels than the dark races. All the villainy the world is governed by originated with the white man, and he has perpetuated it by introducing it among the uncultivated and semi-bar-barians all over the world. They are semi-barbarians, have no knowledge of the Christian religion, or if they have, do not believe the "bad white man."

They do not practice any religious belief. The missionaries and their followers who have visited these islands in their trading vessels have been detected in crime, and the islanders in many instances took revenge, and in return their thatched roof coverings would be burned by the crews of the vessels. The king is said to be the object of their solicitude and belief.

I did not observe any special respect shown the king. The five tribes occupy the island, which is seven miles in circumference, covered with constant verdure, abounding in fine fruit, and the streams and harbor teeming with fish.

Truly, it seemed to be the garden which man first occupied. The pilot told me that the tribes had heard of the American war through him, and he received his intelligence through newspapers which he got from the trading vessels, and the crews told him also of the war. The pilot was my interpreter.

I sent the gig with the pilot and an officer to convey to his Majesty the King of the Lea Harbor tribe our good wishes for his health, peace and prosperity, and to invite him to visit the Shenandoah. In an hour afterwards the gig was on her return escorted by seventy war canoes, each decorated with old faded bunting or colored cotton. In the boat was seated the king, the hereditary prince, and four chiefs, each with a wreath of brilliant flowers upon his head, and an apron made of sea grass falling from the hips half way to the knee. Their bodies glistened in the sunlight, being rubbed with coconut oil to protect them from the sting of the mosquito.

His Majesty came up the side of the Shenandoah very cautiously and, arranging his apron, seated himself between the headboards of the gangway, blocking the passage to the hereditary prince, who was hanging on the vessel's side to a man-rope.

As the pilot was still in the boat, it was impossible to communicate with his Majesty, who was severely dignified in his state of nature. He was motioned to the deck, upon which he stood perfectly erect, looking about unconcerned. After being joined by his retinue, and when they had arranged themselves in their respective positions about their sovereign, I was presented to the king most unceremoniously, the pilot saying, with a motion of his, "That's the king, sir."

His Majesty, with his attendants, were then invited to the cabin and, after the introduction of the pipe and Schiedan schnapps, he became very friendly and seemed greatly impressed by the appearance of the cabin and the various objects which it contained.

The officers who had taken the prizes had captured the mates, the papers, etc., but the masters were absent on a jerry.

An armed boat was kept in readiness to capture the party when it should appear in the harbor. About sunset the party returned, was captured, and conducted to the Shenandoah. The masters of the three vessels which had shown the American flag could give no good reason why their vessels should not be confiscated and themselves held as prisoners, and the master of the vessel which flew the Oahu flag could not produce a bill of sale, nor could he swear to the sale of the vessel.

She bore the name of Harvest of New Bedford, carried an American register, was in charge of the same master who had commanded her on former whaling voyages, and her mates were American. I therefore confiscated her and held her master a prisoner.

The names of the other vessels were the Edward Cory of

148

San Francisco, the Hutor of New Bedford, the Pearl of New London. Taken collectively, their crews numbered one hundred and thirty men and composed of Kanakas. The question of confiscation being settled, and the masters taken care of, it became important to sound his Majesty on the subject of neutrality, and therefore he, with his council, made us a special visit to talk the subject over.

# CHAPTER NINE

On the 3rd day of April his Majesty came on board the Shenandoah accompanied by the hereditary prince and several chiefs. We assembled in the cabin, and the pipe and schnapps having fulfilled their office, the conversation began through the interpreter, who explained the visit of the Shenandoah and the character of the war in which we were engaged.

To all this his Majesty gave a significant grunt while he sipped his schnapps. It was explained to him that the vessels in port belonged to our enemies who had been fighting us for years, killing our people, outraging our country-women, and desolating our homes, and that we were ordered to capture and destroy their vessels whenever and wherever found, and that if the laws of his Majesty would not be violated, the vessels in port would be confiscated, and as there was little contained in them which the Shenandoah required, their contents would be presented to his Majesty to make such use of as he considered proper, and when his tribe had taken all they desired from the ships, I would take them to sea and burn them.

His Majesty, after a short conference with his chiefs (the prince was not consulted) said, "We find nothing conflicting with our laws in what you say. There are shoals in Lea Harbor on which the vessels can be run and then destroyed," and he desired that I would not fire at them, for the shot would go on shore and possibly hurt some of his people.

This was all agreed to, and we commenced removing such things to the Shenandoah as were required. The Harvest was brought alongside the Shenandoah to discharge her fresh water into our tanks, some provisions and five tons of sperm oil which she had on board, and then directed the officers in charge of the prizes to run them on the shoals and allow the natives to take possession until further orders.

Among the stores sent to the Shenandoah were seventy down-east muskets and two dozen infantry coats and pairs of pants, which had been part of her cargo for trade with the island governments. The clothing would suit admirably for a marine guard which I hoped to recruit for the steamer.

It was represented to his Majesty that our "fasts" on shore were very insecure, and that any one disposed to do us mischief could cut them at a moment when the safety of the Shenandoah would be endangered, a flaw of wind could then drive her on the dangerous rock.

His Majesty was desired to station one or more of his warriors to guard the fasts, with orders to shoot any one who should go within prescribed limits to which he replied that he had the warriors but no muskets or ammunition. He was immediately offered the seventy muskets which were taken from the ship Harvest and some ammunition, which he accepted most graciously, and sent his imperial order to station a guard at the fast of the Shenandoah, with authority to kill any one who should venture within the prescribed limits, and his order was instantly obeyed.

Two sentries were armed each with a musket and was posted at the fasts. His Majesty having expressed a desire to examine the Shenandoah with his staff, I gladly accompanied him, but before starting from the cabin I presented

151

him with the sword which had been captured from the schooner Lizzie M. Stacey in the North Atlantic Ocean.

The king had never seen a sword and did not exactly understand its use. He was induced to belt it to his naked waist and one of his staff hung it to the right side. His Majesty eyed the weapon suspiciously, and his expression of countenance conveyed a doubt of the propriety of having it so near his royal person, that it quite overcame my gravity. When told it was proper he should wear the sword during his visit he hesitatingly removed his hand from it.

We had reached the engine room hatch when his Majesty's legs became entangled with his sword as we were in the act of descending. The hereditary prince disengaged him. He objected to descending the ladder with the sword at his side, and the prince was given charge of it.

The machinery excited his surprise and astonishment and found vent in a gutteral cluck of the tongue which each of his staff echoed. He forgot his dignity and resting his royal person against a part of the machinery, became smeared with a white coating used to prevent the machinery from rust. After my return to the cabin he invited me to pay him a visit at the royal residence, which is established at any locality where the fishing is good.

The residence was near the banks of a small river and not far from the margin of the harbor, was built on six piles sufficiently elevated to be beyond the reach of freshets of the river. It was built of cane interlaced with vine and roofed with the broad leaf of the cocoanut tree, and to complete its royal appearance a pair of rickety wooden steps led to the entrance.

A prince met us at the place of landing and conducted us to the residence but did not go in. There was but one room, six by eight, in which the royal family slept, ate, and received visitors. His Majesty's bed was a mat unfolded in a corner upon which he sat, and his queen was sitting near him. He did not rise from the mat when we entered the room nor did his queen in any way acknowledge our presence, and his Majesty beckoned us to seats.

The furniture consisted of two wooden chairs, a box and an old trunk. The latter being softer than the others, was, I suppose, considered the seat of honor, and was offered to me.

The queen was not handsome. She was his second wife. He had desired to marry her before the death of his first queen, but the latter would not consent to the marriage as it would have obliged her to be put aside, there being a law with the tribe that the king can have but one wife. The old queen died very suddenly, no post mortem examination followed, and the king was married upon the following day to his present wife.

The conversation was opened by his Majesty, who asked when the steamer would probably sail and what was to be done with our prisoners. He supposed they would all be put to death, as he considered it right to make such disposition of one's enemies.

I told him they would not be harmed, and that in civilized warfare men destroyed those in armed resistance and paroled the unarmed.

"But," said his Majesty, "war cannot be considered civilized, and those who make war on an unoffending people are a bad people and do not deserve to live."

I told the king I would sail the following day, the 13th of April, and should tell our President of the kind hospitality he had shown to the officers of the Shenandoah and the respect he had paid our flag.

He said, "Tell Jeff Davis he is my brother and a big warrior; that (we are) very poor, but that our tribes are friends. If he will send your steamer for me, I will visit him in his country. I send these two chickens to Jeff Davis (the chickens were dead) and some cocoanuts which he will find good."

His Majesty had no conception of the distance to America and thought, if he thought at all, that within a few days the Shenandoah would convey safely his royal gifts to our President. The muskets were lying about the yard around his house, and a few of the natives were oiling them. He seemed to feel secure from harm now that he was possessed of so many weapons.

When I was about to leave him he rose from his mat and said, "I will go with you to the boat," and when we reached her we found two chickens wrapped in cocoanut leaves and a dozen cocoanuts. Those cocoanuts were a part of the king's revenue. The king's manner was reserved until the schnapps and the pipe warmed him, and then he did not consider it undignified to ask for whatever he fancied and to manifest displeasure if refused.

In this particular, however, he was not unlike his brother sovereigns. He sent on board fruit and fish several times and visited us daily. I gave him a silk scarf which he admired, and he sent me a belt for the shoulders, woven by a native out of fibres of the cocoanut and interwoven with wool procured from the whale vessels which touch there to take in yams, water, hogs and poultry, preparatory to a voyage along the line or in the North Pacific.

The belt is peculiar, exhibiting skill in the art of weaving

154

and taste in blending colors. It is preserved as a memento of the only sovereign who was fearless enough to extend hospitality to a struggling people and to sympathize with a just cause. His nature was not corrupted by politics.

The prizes were run upon the shoals selected by the king, and the canoes surrounding them were handled beautifully. Every movable plank, spar and bulkhead was soon taken on shore for flooring purposes. The sails were removed from the yards and the sailrooms for tents and to be converted into suitable sails for their canoes, and on the vessels floating higher, the canoes were brought to their sides and the natives peeled the copper from their sides and bottom. The natives evidently placed a value on that metal.

I was informed it would be used for pointing spears and arrows, converted into breast-plates, and traded to the neighboring tribes. I saw a great many of the natives, male and female. They are delicate in form and possess all the characteristics of Indians.

Before leaving Lea Harbor, I asked the king's permission to land my prisoners, whom I provided with provisions and two whaleboats. The prisoners preferred to land there rather than be taken to the Island of Guam, and this arrangement suited us best.

The morning of the 13th of April saw all prisoners clear of the Shenandoah and at noon her anchors were tripped and she stood to sea, leaving to the tender care of the king and his tribe one hundred and thirty disappointed whalers who had been in the habit of ill treating and cheating the natives and had introduced diseases among them before unknown to them and for which the poor creatures knew no care.

On leaving Lea Harbor the Shenandoah was continued

under steam, passing to the eastward of the island of Ascension until that island bore per compass S.W. Sail was then made with a fine trade wind and the propeller was raised. When due east from the island, the course was north, leaving to the westward the Ladrone Islands.

The intention was to keep the ship east of Los Jardines, Grampus, and Margaret Islands, and to take her to the westward of Cami-ra, Otra and Mercen Islands.

Never in our various experience of sea life had any of us seen such or more charming weather than we now enjoyed. The sun shone with a peculiar brilliancy and the moon shed that clear, soft light which is found in this locality, in which the heavens seem so distant and so darkly blue, while the vast expanse of ocean was like a great reflecting mirror. The track for vessels bound from San Francisco and many of the ports on the west coast of America to Hong Kong lies between the parallels in north latitude of 17° and 20°. Here the winds are better than are found in a more northerly route, while the track to San Francisco and other ports along the west coast of America from China lies between the parallels of 35° and 45°, because here west winds prevail.

We spent several days·in cruising along those frequented paths, but did not see a sail. The delay was however not without its own reward, for the executive officer, Mr. Whittle, had time to get things in good condition in his department.

After the vessel had reached the parallel of 43° north the weather became cold and foggy and the winds were variable and unsteady, and that ever reliable friend of the sailor, the barometer, indicated atmospheric changes.

The ship was prepared for the change of weather which was rapidly approaching. Soon the ocean was boiling with

156

agitation, and if the barometer had been silent, I would have called it only a furious tide but a dark, then a black cloud, was hurrying towards us from the N. E. and so close did it rest upon the surface of the water that it seemed determined to overwhelm the ship, and there came in it so terrible and violent a wind that the Shenandoah was thrown on her side, and she bounced away as if fright, like the stag from his lair, had started her.

Squall after squall struck her, flash after flash surrounded her, and the thunder rolled in her wake. It was the typhoon. The ocean was as white as the snow and foamed with rage. A new close-reefed main topsail was blown into shreds, and the voice of man was inaudible amid this awful convolution of nature. The violence of the wind was soon over, and the gale abated so that in ten hours thereafter the vessel was standing northward again.

Two days after that fierce blow we encountered another from the same quarter of less violence and of more civility in duration. The weather continued so threatening that it looked impossible for the Shenandoah to get north of the parallel of 45, but the last gale, like its predecessor, had worked to the westward, and the ship began to make her northing again.

On the 17th of May we were north of the parallel of 45 and the weather, though cold, looked more settled, and we took a long breath.

The previous week appeared to have been fuller of trials to us than all our former experience. On the 20th of May the Juril[37] Islands came in sight covered with snow, and on the forenoon of the 21st instant we steamed into the sea of Okhotsk and ran along the coast of Kamchatka under sail.

37 Kuril.

There is a strong current along the Pacific side of these islands setting to the N. E. which clings to the eastern shore on to the Arctic Ocean, and how much further northward man knoweth not.

On the 29th of May we captured and burned the whaling bark Abigail of New Bedford. When she was discovered, the Shenandoah was skirting an extensive field of floe ice, and beyond, in the direction of Greer (or Shantarski)[38] Island, was another. The sail was seen standing towards us and I therefore awaited her arrival and learned from her that the master mistook us for a Russian provision vessel going to the settlement of Okhotsk to supply Russian officials.

Several of the Abigail's crew joined the Shenandoah, and among them a New Bedford man, a genuine down-easter. The master was frightfully astonished at his situation and could hardly realize his misfortune. He had before fallen into the clutches of the Alabama, and his vessel had been destroyed, and although he had now come almost out of the world to make a paying voyage, he had again failed.

He had been away from home three years when we took him. One of the mates who was not sorry for the disaster which had befallen his late master said to him,

"You are more fortunate in picking up Confederate cruisers than whales. I will never again go with you, for if there is a cruiser out, you will find her."

I continued as far as the Chi-jinskiki Bay, but found it so full of ice the steamer could not be entered. I then stood along the land of eastern Siberia as far as Tausk Bay, when she was forced away by the ice, and I left for Shantaski (Shantarski) Island, but I found ice in such quantities before we reached the 150° meridian of east longitude that

[38] Shantarskie.

158

she was forced to the southward finding ice in almost every direction and apparently closing on her.

The situation caused anxiety of mind, and I solved the seamanship problem before us. The scene was cold, the mercury several degrees below zero, the ice varied in thickness from fifteen to thirty feet and, although not very firm, was sufficiently so to injure the Shenandoah if we were not very careful. I wanted to reach Shantarski Island (called by whalers Greer Island) for there is fishing there and in the bays southwest of it. Within twenty days the Shenandoah had run from the tropics into snow and ice, from excessive heat to this cold climate, and yet there was no illness more severe than colds from which we soon recovered.

The cabin had been without a stove, and the Abigail supplied the deficiency. To prevent sickness, an order forbidding unnecessary exposure of the crew was given, and the vessel was kept under easy sail.

The men were required by our very excellent Surgeon Lining to clothe themselves warmly and keep themselves dry. Extra rations of hot coffee and grog were served at regular hours, and the surgeon, with his efficient assistant, Dr. McNulty, inspected the food for the crew before and after it was prepared. Indeed the surgeon cannot be recommended too highly for his discretion in preserving the sanitary condition of the Shenandoah. The gales during the summer months north of the parallel of 40° are frequently of few hours duration and move with excessive velocity, testing the strength of everything within their path.

The Shenandoah met several of those gales in the Okhotsk Sea. The damage from these gales is much increased by the heavy ice which a vessel is likely to be driven on and wrecked. We encountered the first one of those gales to

159

windward of twenty miles of floe ice, and if we had been lying to with the ice under our lea, the Shenandoah would probably have been lost with her entire crew.

It became imperatively necessary to relieve the ship of her perilous situation. She was run a little distance from and along the floe until a passage was seen from aloft through it with open water beyond. Into this passage she was entered and in a short time she was lying to under close reefed sails with the floe to windward, and this was the solution of that seamanship problem alluded to a little time before, for our dreaded enemy was now become our best friend, the fury of the sea was expended on it and not against the Shenandoah. It was a breakwater for the ship.

She laid perfectly easy, the water was as smooth as a pond, while the seas on the weather edge of the floe broke furiously, throwing sheets of water twenty feet high, to all appearances a fog bank.

It was so far away we could only hear the hurrying of wind as it piped louder and carried in it a penetrating mist. The Shenandoah being relieved of the threatened danger, the next thought was to prevent her from going into the ice during the thick weather, which now came on in fine rain and sleet. The wind was bitter cold, turning the rain into ice and forming a crust everywhere. The braces, blocks, yards, sails and all the running rigging was perfectly coated with ice from a half to two inches thick, so that it was impossible to use the braces and icicles of great length and size hung from every portion of the rigging.

The gale had passed over, and it was calm, the clouds were exhausted, the rosy tints of morn opened upon a scene of enchantment, and when the sunlight burst on us, the flash and sparkle from truck to deck, from bowsprit to

160

topsail, awakened exclamations of enthusiastic delight over the fair ship.

The disposition was evidently not to disturb, but leave to enjoyment the crystal mantle of the Shenandoah. Finally the crew was sent aloft with billets of wood to dislodge the ice and free the running rigging. The large icicles falling from aloft rendered the deck dangerous to move upon, and it soon became covered with clear, beautiful ice, which was removed to the tanks, casks, and every vessel capable of receiving it.

# CHAPTER TEN

A supply of several thousand gallons of drinking water was most acceptable, for it saved consumption of coal in condensing. As soon as the rigging was clear of ice so that the braces could traverse the blocks without danger of chafe, warps were run out on the floe and grapnels hooked to large blocks of ice, and the ship was gradually worked out of a field of ice into which she had worked during the calm. One gathers experience under certain circumstances, and becomes accustomed to situations which create anxiety at first.

It was evident from the quantity of drift ice in view that the flow was westward, and to continue the ship in that direction would be useless. She was therefore run to the eastward and after knocking about till the 14th of June, I left the sea of Okhotsk and entered the North Pacific Ocean by the fiftieth parallel passage of Amphitrite Strait, and steering N. E. with a cracking southwester after us.

When I gave the course N. E. it was to run the ship midway of the most western of the Aleutian and the most eastern of Komandorski Islands,[39] because currents about islands are irregular in direction as well as in force. In a few hours after leaving Amphitrite Strait the wind hauled more to the south and then east of south, producing a condensation of the atmosphere which closed around the Shenandoah an impenetrable mist.

I continued on the course for twenty-four hours, and

[39] Komandorskie.

162

the wind having hauled still more to the eastward, I deemed it prudent to give a course of E. N. E., because we were without solar or other observations, and the wind would give the current a set to the N. W. which if not considered, would force the ship too much away from a direct course, and perhaps place her uncomfortably near the Komandorski Island. I therefore allowed two points for drift in a northwest direction. At the end of the next twenty-four hours we were again without solar or other observations, but I knew from the dead reckoning the ship must be near the passage. The wind had drawn more from the eastward and the ship was heading more northerly.

During the afternoon the wind fell light from northeast, which was a pretty sure sign of the nearness of land, and with that change of wind the fog lifted a little to tell the mariner of his danger, when the cry of land O was heard from the lookouts. At intervals it could be seen ahead, distant not more than four or five miles.

The ship was put on the port tack, having just wind enough to turn round and away from the land. The wind died away entirely leaving a fog denser than ever. The land that had been seen was Copper Island. The ship was thirty-seven miles out of her reckoning, notwithstanding the large allowance made for drift, etc.

Steam was ordered, sails were furled, and we entered Behring Sea on the afternoon of the 16th of June, 1865. The cruising in Behring Sea under sail was not of the most delightful character. Changes of weather were more sudden, and although fogs did not last so long as in the Sea of Okhotsk, they were more frequent.

We made Cape Navarin on the 21st of June, and finding a current setting to the N. E. and soon after seeing blubber we concluded the whale vessels southwest of us were cutting out, and steam was ordered. This calculation was correct, for the steamer had not gone in a southwest direction more than an hour when the masthead lookouts cried sail O! Two sail were in sight.

The Shenandoah gave chase and soon came up with the whalers, William Thompson and Euphrates, both New Bedford, and before the prize crews could be placed on board of those vessels another sail was reported. A breeze had sprung up and to work quickly was all important. Leaving the prize officers in charge of the vessels and having their masters on board of the Shenandoah, we started in chase of and overhauled the British bark Robert L. Towns of Sydney. Her master was anxious to know the name of our ship, and I gave to him Petropauluski. The William Thompson was the largest whale ship out of New Bedford, and after the removal of the prisoners and nautical instruments both vessels were set on fire. Those vessels had been very successful in fishing.

The following day five vessels were discovered near a large body of ice, and I stood for them, hoisted the American flag, and communicated with the nearest one, which was the whale ship Milo of New Bedford.

The Shenandoah passed close under her stern and the master was invited to come on board with his papers. He complained, and was surprised to learn the nationality of the steamer, and said he had heard of her being in Australia, but did not expect to see her in the Arctic Ocean.

I asked for news. He said the war was over. I then asked for documentary evidence. He had none, but "believed the war was over." I replied that was not satisfactory, but that if he could produce any reliable evidence, I would receive it. He answered "that he could not produce any reliable evidence" and then said he had taken the steamer to be a telegraph vessel which they had been expecting to lay a cable between Russian America and Eastern Siberia.

He was informed that I was willing to ransom the Milo if he accepted the conditions. He reflected a moment and said, "I will give bond and receive all prisoners."

I received his register and bond, and directed him to return to the Milo and send all his boats with full crews to the Shenandoah, and to back his foretopsail.

The Milo boats came to the Shenandoah and I steamed in pursuit of two vessels which seemed to be in communication. I resorted to that stratagem with the Milo to prevent her escape, for if I had not removed her crew, what was there to prevent an escape of some of the vessels?

A breeze had sprung up, the vessels had taken alarm, and we knew the work before us required promptitude. Their masters had been in communication and were then entering their vessels in the floe. The Shenandoah was run close to and parallel with the ice and separated the vessels, each being about a mile distant from us. I then fired a gun at the furthest one which made her heave-to. Her consort then tacked and stood out of the ice for the Siberian coast with a good wind.

I fired a second gun at the vessel which had hove to, and the master received it as an order to come out of the floe and submit to the fate which awaited him. This bark proved to be the Sophia Thornton. Her master and mates were received on board the Shenandoah.

The officer in charge of the prize, Lieutenant Scales, was directed to communicate with the Milo and command the master to keep company with the Sophia Thornton, which vessel was ordered to follow the Shenandoah. The Milo could not escape because she was without a crew and her register, and as she had given bond for $50,000 there was no inducement to do so.

The Jerah Swift, which was a fast bark, had made her escape with a good breeze and wanted to reach the marine league of the coast of Siberia. We chased her for three hours before getting in shelling distance of her, but Captain Williams, who made every effort to save his bark, saw the folly of exposing the crew to a destructive fire and yielded to his misfortune with a manly and becoming dignity.

When the boarding officer, Lieutenant Lee, reached the Swift, he found her captain and crew with their personal effects packed and ready to leave the bark in her boats for the Shenandoah, and the Jerah Swift was in flames twenty minutes thereafter.

The prisoners were all transferred to the Milo, and she was furnished with supplies from the stores of the Sophia Thornton, and I gave her master a certificate stating that I held the ship's register. She was sent to San Francisco that the Richmond Government should know of our whereabouts.

Captain Williams stated to the officers that "he did not believe the war was over," but felt certain the South would yield eventually.

On the 23rd of June we captured the brig Susan Abigail of San Francisco with California papers containing a number of despatches, and among them other statements contained in them was the announcement that the Southern Government had been removed to Danville, and that the greater part of the army of Virginia had joined General Johnston in North Carolina where an indecisive battle had been fought with General Sherman.

166

They also stated that at Danville a proclamation was issued by President Davis, announcing that the war would be carried on with renewed vigor, and exhorting the people of the South to bear up heroically under their calamities.

The master of the Susan Abigail was questioned as to the general opinion in San Francisco about the condition of American affairs, and he said, "Opinion is divided as to the ultimate result of the war. For the present the North has the advantage, but how it will all end no one can know, and as to the newspapers they are not reliable."

The Susan Abigail gave the latest information from America and she fell into our hands before she had seen any other vessel, indeed the Shenandoah was the first vessel her master had seen since he had left San Francisco.

The Susan Abigail was destroyed. Three of the Susan Abigail's crew joined the Shenandoah, which was good evidence at least that they did not believe the war had ended. They were not pressed to ship, but sought service under our flag.

The brig was on a trading voyage for furs, gold quartz and whale bone, which her master got of the native Indians in exchange for bright articles of apparel, tobacco and whiskey.

The Shenandoah was now north of the Island of St. Lawrence, under sail, with fires banked. Several Esquimaux canoes with natives from the island visited us, and our crew struck up a brisk trade with them for furs and walrus tusks. It was interesting and curious, as we had no means of communication with them except through signs.

On the 24th of June I put the Shenandoah under steam in chase of the General Williams of New London. We captured and burned her.

On the 26th of June we had chased and captured the following six American whale vessels, and burned the whole of them except the General Pike, who was ransomed. Barks, vix., Wm. C. Nye, Nimrod, Catharine, Isabella and Gipsy. The General Pike had lost her master, and the mate was in charge of her, who asked as a special favor to be allowed to ransom her.

He said, "If you ransom the Pike, her owner will think me so fortunate in saving her that it will give me a claim on them for the command."

All the prisoners were sent to the General Pike, and she was given a certificate for San Francisco. On the 27th of June the Shenandoah was under sail with a head wind. Things had gotten lively, and we were very interested in our friends, who had left the South Pacific to escape us.

Eleven sail were in sight and all to windward. We felt sure of their nationality, but to attempt their capture while there was wind would result in the loss of a part of them. We lowered the smoke stack and continued in the rear of the eleven, keeping a close luff, and retarding our progress as much as possible, so as to arouse no suspicions amongst them.

On the 28th, at 10:30 A.M. a calm ensued. The game were collected in East Cape Bay, and the Shenandoah entered the bay under the American flag with a fine pressure of steam on. Every vessel present hoisted the American flag. We had heard of the whale ship James Murray off the Island of Ascension, and after reaching Behring Sea had heard again of her and also of the death of her master, whose widow and two little children were on board.

While our boats were being armed preparatory to taking possession of the prizes, a boat from the whale ship Brunswick came to the steamer, and the mate in charge of the boat, ignorant of our true nationality, represented that the Brunswick had struck a piece of ice a few hours before which left a hole in her starboard bow twenty inches below the water line, and asked for assistance.

To their application we replied, "We are very busy now, but in a little while we will attend to you."

The mate thanked us, and he was asked which of the vessels was the James Murray. He pointed her out. The Brunswick laid on her side, her casks of oil floating her well up, and her master, seeing his vessel a hopeless wreck, had offered his oil to any one purchaser among the masters of the other vessels at twenty cents per gallon.

The Shenandoah being in position to command the fleet with her guns, hoisted our flag, and the armed boats (we had only five of them) were despatched to take possession of the vessels with orders to send their masters with the ship's papers to the Shenandoah.

The American flags were hauled down instantly. The eleventh still hung to the vessel's gaff, and seeing someone on her deck with a gun, an officer was sent to capture her and send the master to the Shenandoah. That vessel was the bark Favorite of New Haven, and her master was drunk from too free a use of intoxicating liquor.

The bark Favorite was without a register liable to seizure in time of profound peace, by any police of the ocean. The hurry and confusion upon the decks of those vessels, the consternation among the crews may be imagined.

The boarding officer of the James Murray sent her mate to represent the very distressed condition of the wife and children of the late captain, that the poor widow had the remains of her husband on board preserved in whiskey. A

169

messenger was sent to the unhappy widow to inform her she and the children were under the protection of the Shenandoah and no harm would come to her or the vessel, that the men of the South did not make war on women and children.

The following vessels were burned. Ships, Hillman, Nassau, Brunswick, Isaac Howland; barks, Waverly, Martha, Favorite, Covington, Congress. I ransomed the James Murray and the Milo. Within twelve hours after these vessels were discovered, nine of them were enveloped in flames. The crews of those vessels amounted to 336 men; among them we received nine men, all intelligent soldiers, men who had been taught to respect military authority and who knew how to use the Enfield rifle. The enlistment of those men in the Confederate service is evidence that if they had heard any report of the military failure of the South, they considered it so unreliable as not to hinder their seeking service in the Shenandoah.

It cannot be supposed that those men would embark in a cause which they believed to be lost. No, the failure of the South to establish her independence was not known to any one who fell into our hands, nor was it even surmised, for those waters are so removed from the ordinary channels of communication that it was simply impossible for authentic tidings of the progress of the American war to have reached so remote a part of the world between the time of the actual overthrow of that government and the capture of those vessels.

One of the masters of those vessels was brother to the down-easter who joined the Shenandoah in the Okhotsk Sea. When the brothers met, they shook hands, but the master pretended great indignation on learning that his brother had taken service in the Shenandoah. After a short

170

conversation between the brothers the master was of the opinion "that it is right to make a living."

The ransomed ships were furnished with certificates stating why they were without registers, and they were supplied with an outfit and ordered to depart. An occasional explosion on board some of the burning vessels betrayed the presence of gunpowder or other combustible matter. A liquid flame now and then pursued an inflammable substance which had escaped from the sides to the water, and the horizon was illuminated with a fiery glare presenting a picture of indescribable grandeur, while the water was covered with black smoke mingled with flakes of fire.

Leaving this scene of destruction, the Shenandoah's prow was turned northward amid snow and icebergs until she reached latitude 66°40′ when, in consequence of her great length, the immensity of the ice and floes, the danger of being shut up in the Arctic Ocean for several months, I was obliged to turn her prow southward and reached East Cape just in time to slip by the Diomedes when a vast field of floe ice was closing the strait.

The steamer entered the floe and caution was observed to save her from injury, for now she pressed her way through the extremest danger which, though it had become familiar to us was most uncomfortable and alarming. The sun was in his highest northern declination, and it was perpetual daylight, when he sank below the northern horizon a golden fringe marked his course until his pale and cheerless face came again frosted from icebergs and snows.

When the Shenandoah reached the Island of St. Lawrence there was a fine northwest wind. Sail was made, and the propeller triced up. While to the westward of that island, the ships making six knots per hour, a dense fog came on which so perfectly cut off the view from the officer of the watch that he found the vessel in pilot ice, which is certain evidence of large bodies of ice being near, and before he could shorten sail sufficiently, the ship ran into a large and dangerous floe.

Mr. Lee braced the sails aback, she gathered sternboard quickly, which was counteracted by counterbracing the yards. While going astern the pressure of the rudder against the ice under her counter parted one of the teter [*sic*] chains. All sail was taken in, and while that duty was going on, the steamer was in danger. Sail being taken in, she laid comfortably enough in the ice and blocked in. Warps and grapnels were run out as on a previous occasion, and she was swung in the right direction and with strong rope mats over her prow (which extended on either side to the fore channels) to protect her from bruises. Steam was gently applied and with a large block of ice resting against her cutwater she pushed it along to open a passage, and in this way we worked the Shenandoah for hours until she gained open water.

# CHAPTER ELEVEN

It was now time to run the steamer out of these waters into more open seas, for if intelligence of my movements had reached any of the enemy's cruisers belonging to the squadrons of the Pacific or Asiatic Station from any source, or specially from the ransomed ships which were sent from Behring Sea, it would have been easy for them to blockade the Shenandoah or force her into action. To avoid such a result was my imperative duty, for it would not be wise to risk the steamer in a contest in which, even if successful, she would be materially injured, and perhaps rendered unfit for service until taken into a port for repairs. We knew but too well the character of the neutrality of the first naval power of the earth to suppose that any government bordering on the Pacific coast would endanger its existence by receiving a Confederate cruiser for repairs and thus incur the displeasure of the worst government under the sun. Since the great powers of Europe shrunk from such a responsibility, what was to be expected from weaker ones? Two days before the Shenandoah left Behring Sea a black fog closed upon us and shut out from our view the heavens and all things terrestrial. Still we pressed on towards the Aleutian Islands, which stretches from the Alaska Peninsula in a semicircular course towards the coast of Kamchatka. A glance at a map representing that part of the world shows alternate land and water for a distance of twenty degrees of longitude, when the dead reckoning gave to the ship a position near

173

the Amoutchta Pass, through which I intended the Shenandoah should enter the North Pacific Ocean.

The fog continued thick and black, but the ship dashed along trusting to accuracy of judgment and a hope that the fog would lift so that the land could be seen four or five miles off should I fail to strike the center of the passage.

It would have been a mistake to stop steaming or to run on a circle because of thick weather in a sea and near islands where currents are irregular in force and direction. The drift of the ship would perhaps have proved more fatal than running on a direct course from last observation. It was preferred to run the Shenandoah for the pass, assuming that three sights taken near noon the day before, when the fog cleared for a moment, gave an approximate position to the ship, which partially corroborated the dead reckoning, although no two of them agreed.

By taking a middle course for the centre of the pass it would be more prudent to go ahead than to wait for clear weather. When the ship was believed to be about the centre of the pass land was seen from both beams, and the position of the Shenandoah was ascertained by taking cross bearings. The feeling of safety when a danger is over is truly delightful.

Again in the North Pacific with fine weather and the Aleutian Islands astern, I looked back in thankfulness towards those seas in which we had seen hard and dangerous service, and I felt a sensation of freedom on that vast outstretched water before us, no longer dreading the cry from the masthead of "ice ahead." We had run from gloomy fogs into a bright, cheerful, sparkling ocean, and as soon as a hot sun thawed the frosty timbers and rigging of ship and man, we should feel ourselves more than a match for anything we might meet under canvas.

174

It was the 5th of July when the Aleutian Islands were lost to view and the craft made for the parallel where west winds would hasten her over to the coast of California, for I had matured plans for entering the harbor of San Francisco and laying that city under contribution.[40]

The newspapers which were captured gave intelligence of the disposition of the American naval vessels and I was not unfamiliar with their commanding officers or their sagacity. In the harbor of San Francisco was an ironclad commanded by Charles McDougal, an old and familiar shipmate of mine. We had been together in the Saginaw and McDougal was fond of his ease. I did not feel that he would be in our way, any officer of the Shenandoah was more than a match for Mc in activity and will. There was no other vessel of war there, as I concluded from San Francisco newspaper reports, and to enter the port after night and collide with the iron ram was easy enough, and with our force thrown upon the ironclad's deck and in possession of her hatches, no life need have been lost. Mc. could have been with the officers secured, and e'er daylight came, both batteries could have been sprung on the city and my demands enforced.

Prudence indicated communicating with a vessel recently from San Francisco before attempting the enterprise. The Shenandoah moved gently along with light winds or dashed before occasional gales until we reached the meridian of 129 W. when with the north wind that sweeps down the California coast her course was parallel with the land and we kept a sharp lookout, for we were then in waters frequented by the enemy's vessels. On the 2nd of August I or-

[40] This was following Bulloch's plan of sending the rams to raze West Coast cities.

dered steam in chase of a bark, and in a short time we came up with and boarded the British bark Barracouta of Liverpool from San Francisco. The following extract is taken from the remarks in our log book, made by the lieutenant of the watch:

> Having received by the British bark Barracouta the sad intelligence of the overthrow of the Confederate Government, all attempts to destroy the shipping or property of the United States will cease from this date, in accordance with which the First Lieutenant Wm. C. Whittle, Jr., received an order from the commander to strike below the battery and disarm the ship and crew.　　D. M. Scales.

My life had been checkered from the dawn of my naval career and I had believed myself schooled to every sort of disappointment, but the dreadful issue of that sanguinary struggle was the bitterest blow, because unexpected, I had yet encountered. It cast a gloom over the whole ship and did occupy my thoughts. I had, however, a responsibility of the highest nature resting upon me in deciding the course we should pursue, which involved not only our personal honor, but the honor of the flag entrusted to us which had walked the waters fearlessly and in triumph.

At the blush of surrender of the Shenandoah I saw the propriety of running her for a European port which, though it involved a voyage of seventeen thousand miles, it was the right thing to do. A long gauntlet to run, to be sure, but why not succeed in baffling observation or pursuit. The enemy had gloated over his success and would, like a gorged serpent, lie down to rest.

The Shenandoah up to that time had made more than forty thousand miles without an accident. I felt sure a search would be made for her in the North Pacific and that to run the ship south was important to all concerned. Some of the people expressed a desire that I should take the Shenandoah to Australia or New Zealand or any near port rather than attempt to reach Europe. There seemed however to me no other course to pursue but the one I had decided upon, and I considered it due the integrity of all to reject anything and everything like flinching under the severe trial imposed upon us. It was my duty as a man and a commanding officer to be careful of the honor as well as the welfare of the one hundred and thirty-two men placed in my hands.

The run down to Cape Horn was expeditious, and before we reached the pitch of the cape we passed several American vessels bound to the west. One vessel only was standing in the direction we steered and she was an English passenger vessel of large tonnage who ran away from the Shenandoah.

I attribute the apparent slowness of the steamer to the condition of her copper and foulness of her bottom, and it was an uncomfortable thing to know that it might require more than all her fleetness now to escape a Federal cruiser.

If the Barracouta had been an American vessel I would have destroyed her, would have rejected her advices, because the Washington Government, by forging official reports (for instance the naval report with Mr. Mallory's name attached to it) had made it impossible to believe their papers. It was a part of their system of carrying on the war. They openly avowed it as a legitimate means of strategy and called it "moral strategy" as opposed to "military strategy." Mr. Seward used it in his correspondence with foreign governments and Mr. Stanton had employed it to impose on the credulity of the people of the north with regard to the reports of the battles.

I had not left the South Atlantic Ocean when the cavalier

Stanton ordered the arrest and imprisonment of Mrs. Waddell because she was the wife of the 'pirate of the Shenandoah.' My wife was imprisoned, and done with the knowledge of President Lincoln and Secretary Seward.

If it be true that Mr. Stanton committed suicide, no wonder he cut his unhaltered throat, his horrible crimes could in no way be expiated so well as in his violation of the sixth commandment. Is suicide murder?

The wind was northwest on the Pacific side of Tierra del Fuego, and for hours before the Shenandoah doubled Cape Horn she ran at the rate of fifteen miles per hour. She passed to the eastward of the Cape on the 16th of September when she took a northeast gale which forced her to west longitude of 24°40′ before she reached the parallel of 40°S. She passed near the Shag Rocks in cold and boisterous weather. Day after day icebergs and savage blocks of ice came near us. We were without a moon to shed her cheerful light upon our desolate path and the wind was so fierce that the ship's speed could not be reduced below five knots per hour.[41] It was more prudent to go ahead than to heave to, for we were without observations for several days and in an easterly current.

Some of the icebergs were castellated and resembled fortifications with sentinels on guard, but although the nights were dark we escaped injury. The struggles of our ship were but typical of the struggles that filled our breasts upon learning that we were alone on that friendless deep without a home or country, our little crew all that were left of the thousands who had sworn to defend that country or die with her, and there were moments when we would have deemed that a friendly gale which would have buried our sorrowful

[41] *Sic!*

178

hearts and the beautiful Shenandoah in those dark waters.

What a contrast to those gay hopes and proud aspirations with which we had entered upon the cruise. How eager we had been to court danger. Now gloomily and cautiously we avoided recognition. The very ship seemed to have partaken our feelings and no longer moved with her accustomed swiftness. The steamer's course was northward with a good S. E. wind, and she crossed her outward track on the parallel of 30°S.

Applications were here made to take the ship to Cape Town, and I declined to do so, keeping to the east of the 30th meridian and crossing the line on the 11th of October. The Shenandoah fell in with a great many sail but kept at a polite distance from them, working her way along under sail through calms and light airs. In latitude 10° N. we took the trades.

On the afternoon of the 25th of October when she had nearly run out of the trades and her sails fanning her along, a masthead lookout cried sail O! The cry sail O! brought many to their feet who were indulging repose, and their anxious glances evinced their state of mind, for if a Federal cruiser was to be found anywhere she would be in that region of ocean. Glasses swept the northern horizon in search of the sail, but she was visible only from aloft. A quarter master was sent aloft with orders to communicate all he could ascertain from the appearance of the sail.

He made the survey and reported her under short sail with the mainsail hauled up or furled. That from the spread of her canvas and masts she looked like a steamer, and that she was standing a little more to the east of north than the Shenandoah was heading. The sun was thirty minutes high and the sky was cloudless. We could make no change in the course of the ship or the quantity of sail she carried, for to arouse the suspicions of the sail might expose the Shenandoah to investigation. Whatever she was she had seen our ship and might be waiting to speak her. The Shenandoah was perceptibly shortening the distance between herself and the sail, and there was danger that she would approach too near during daylight for she could already be seen from our deck. The propeller had been lowered to impede her progress, but the favoring night seemed to come on more slowly than I had ever before known it.

The situation was one of intense suspense, for our security, if any remained, depended on a strict adherence to the course we were pursuing. Any deviation from that would probably be noticed from the sail. We could not reduce sail to lessen her progress through the water. There was but one hope, and that was in a drag, two ends of a hawser made fast and the bite thrown overboard would retard in some degree her progress. After the sun had gone

"Not as in northern climes obscurely bright,
But one unclouded blaze of living light."   B.

I directed another observation of the sail from aloft. She was reported to be a steamer and no doubt a man of war. When darkness closed between us we could not have been more than three miles distant. The Shenandoah's head was turned south and steam was ordered. At nine o'clock while our sails were being furled the moon rose and the surface presented a little before by the Shenandoah being greatly diminished by that maneuver it would be difficult to find where she lay.

The Cardiff coal makes a white vapor which could not be seen two hundred yards off, and now that the engines

180

were working and the steamer heading east, we had all the advantages to be expected. It was the first time our ship had been under steam since crossing the line in the Pacific Ocean, indeed the fires were not lighted during a distance of over thirteen thousand miles. The Shenandoah was five hundred miles southeast of the Azores, and if there was an American cruiser in that locality on the 25th day of October, 1865, we were probably in sight of each other. I have been told that the U. S. steamer Saranac, Captain Walke, was probably the vessel.

I continued an east course for fifteen miles and then stood north for one hundred miles, when a strong southwest gale dashed her along to within seven hundred miles of the port of Liverpool. A calm ensued, leaving us in sight of eleven sail and all of them agreeably distant from us.

The ship was continued under sail during the daylight, because if we had gotten up steam it would have been observed, and as each sail was ignorant of the character of the other, it would have directed attention to the steamer, and one of them might have been a Federal cruiser.

As soon as night received us in her friendly folds steam was applied and we were off for St. George's Channel. The weather continued calm and beautiful, and I entered the channel on the 5th of November, just 122 days from the Aleutian Islands.

The chronometers had not been rated since we left Melbourne, and we had not seen land since we had left the Aleutian Islands, and yet we could not have made a more beautiful land fall. The beacon in St. George's Channel was seen where and at the time looked for. I received a pilot after midnight, and when he was informed it was the Shenandoah he exclaimed, "I was reading a few days ago of your being in the Arctic Ocean."

I asked for the news from America. His statements corroborated the Barracouta's intelligence. I desired the pilot to take the ship into the Mersey that I might communicate with her British Majesty's Government.

On the morning of the 6th of November, 1865, the Shenandoah steamed up the River Mersey in a thick fog under the Confederate flag, and the pilot had orders to anchor her near H. M. ship-of-the-line Donegal, Captain Paynter, R. N.

Shortly after we anchored a lieutenant from the Donegal visited us to ascertain the name of the vessel and gave me official intelligence of the termination of the American war. He was polite. The flag was then hauled down.

All on board were confined to the vessel by the authorities. We were informed that everybody must remain on board, and an order to that effect was given. Some persons voluntarily left the vessel with no intention to desert, which was discovered by the English lieutenant-commander, whose gunboat was lashed alongside the Shenandoah at the request of the American minister to prevent her from getting to sea. "How absurd!" the lieutenant said pleasantly, "I don't care if the lads do take a run on shore after night." I expressed regret to learn that anyone had done so.

"Oh," said he, "you won't leave the vessel, I know, so it don't matter about the lads going on a bit of a lark."

He several times invited me on board of his gunboat, but I invariably refused to leave the vessel. I could leave her in only one of two ways. Either by the acceptance of the surrender of the Shenandoah, leaving me at liberty to go when I pleased, or I must be taken out of her a prisoner.

Captain Paynter visited me several times and gratified

182

me by expressing his approval of the good conduct exhibited by those who had so recently been under my command under circumstances so painful.

"It is," said he, "the result of a good discipline and confidence in your rectitude."

Before reaching Liverpool there was money on board of the ship which was captured prior to the surrender of the Southern armies and other money which had been captured after the surrender of the Southern armies. The former I directed to be divided among the officers and crew according to the law on the subject of prize money, of which I declined to receive the portion which I would be entitled to, and it was divided among the officers and crew with the rest of the money.[42] That which was captured after the surrender of the Southern armies was surrendered to Paymaster Robert W. Warwick, H. M. ship Donegal, and a receipt taken, of which the following is a copy:

> Received of Captain James I. Waddell a bag said to contain $820.28, consisting of mixed gold and silver, as per papers annexed to bag.
>
> H. Lloyd, Clerk.
>
> Shenandoah, Liverpool, November 8, 1865.
> Witness to delivery:
>
> Robert W. Warwick,
> Paymaster H. M. Ship Donegal.

By some accident we were left on salt provisions for two days our friends on shore not knowing that there was any

---

[42] Hunt, in his memoirs, charges Waddell with keeping back some of the money Bulloch sent him for the officers. Bulloch does not make mention of this in his memoirs. He has only high praise for Waddell. As the only officer who broke his word and fled the ship when she was returned to Liverpool, Hunt and his charges have to be viewed with suspicion.

communication with us. On the 10th of November, 10 officers, 14 acting appointments, and 100 men who constituted the ship's company, were unconditionally released. My tumblers, decanters, and bedding, with a few trophies from the islands, were presented to the Lieutenant-commander as a souvenir of our acquaintance.

The late officers and men of the Shenandoah were taken to Great George landing in Liverpool at the expense of H. M. Government. Our thanks are due Captain Paynter, R. N., for his kindness to us during our imprisonment in the Mersey, and for the manly interest he manifested. The Shenandoah was actually cruising eight months in search of the property of the enemy, during which time she made 38 captures, of which she released six on bond and destroyed thirty-two of them.[43] She was the only vessel which carried the flag of the South around the world.

She carried it six months after the war was over and she was surrendered to the British nation. The last gun in defense of the South was fired from her deck, and that gun was fired by South Carolina's gallant son, Lieutenant John Grimball. She ran a distance of 58,000 miles and met with no serious injury during a cruise of thirteen months. Her anchors were on her bows for eight months. She never abandoned a chase and was second to no other cruiser, not excepting the celebrated Alabama.

I claim for her officers and men a triumph over their enemies and over every obstacle which they encountered. And to the executive officer, Lieutenant W. C. Whittle, I

[43] A study of the quartermaster reports of western frontier army posts at the end of the war shows that the *Shenandoah*'s virtual wiping out of the whaling fleet was largely responsible for the rise in popularity of the cheaper coal oil.

express my thanks for his faithful and watchful discharge of duty.

One word before I close to those noble men who were officers under my command. The circumstance of age and rank, not superior merit or greater devotion to our cause, made me their commander. For thirteen long months we were thrown into a connection so close that the narrative I write seems rather a souvenir of our intercourse than a statement of historical events. To each and all of them I shall ever feel bound by strong ties of personal and professional attachment.

We received our little vessel with the same high hopes. We encountered in our cruise the same dangers. And we were finally overwhelmed in the same great sorrow in the loss of our country.

Gentlemen by family and cultivation, naval officers by preference and education, at a time of life when men can with difficulty break old habits and adopt a new profession, they found themselves exiles in a foreign land without a home or a government, and by the ungenerous conduct of the U. S. authorities debarred from all the avenues of professional advancement in foreign countries. Some of them have sought to establish themselves in South America and others in Mexico. Wherever they may be, or in whatever pursuit engaged, I pray to feel that although their names may not be preserved by the naval records of a government, that their late commander in the Confederate service, whose duty it was by position and circumstance to judge them, has borne testimony to their having merited by their devotion and conduct the grateful regard and remembrance of the people whom it was their pride and happiness to serve.

The navy, like the flag it bore, though dead, yet will it live, and I will write about those things which occupied the thoughts of my boyhood, grew with my growth into manhood, and have ever fascinated my understanding.

The personnel of the Confederate navy has written its history in human gore, and I need not here descant on the odds it met, the places where conflicts and results occurred, but like its heroism, so has it become history, that it gave to the naval powers of earth the armor plated fighting ship.

The illustrious names which adorn its record, constitute a navy, without such spirits iron and wooden ships of war mean nothing. It is the inspiration of the Godlike soul which throws light into such material, and those names go down to coming generations, a people's pride, a people's glory, and a people's history.

The cruising vessels of the Confederate States were intended to operate against the enemy's commerce. They were few, slightly built, and swift, and those vessels took absolute possession of the waters of the world, driving, without opposion, the enemy's mercantile marine from the ocean, that were so fortunate to escape capture into port, and even there they were captured.

As champions of a cause which commended itself, even to those whose political instincts it offended, tribute has been offered to their patriotism and to their country's chivalry. No greater compliment could be paid them than the enemy's running abuse for twenty years. It has been charged to them that they were content with burning merchantmen and destroying the commerce of the enemy, and as they did only what every belligerent power is most ambitious of doing to its opponent, the charge is a testimony to their activity and skill.

186

They may well be excused for using a weapon that their enemy had furnished them. If privateering, as they still will have it, was the vice of the Confederates, then the Federals are responsible for having sanctioned it. If it was the one engine of war which harrassed them most, then they reaped the penalty of having fabricated it. It is well known that when Europe conspired to put down the system, America refused to divest warfare of one of its most cruel accessories.

Sum up the offenses against civilization of which both sides were guilty and then see which is the greater criminal. Have the people who speak of the captains of those cruisers as pirates ever heard of the theft of the Florida?

The Federal Government distinguished itself famously in this class of transactions, but did it ever surpass the outrage in Brazilian waters on the 4th of October, 1864? Did it ever give a more conspicuous exhibition of the code of law and honor which ruled it and which its apologists affected to despise in their opponents?

We all recollect the tale of treachery. The Florida arrived at Bahia Brazil on the 4th of October, 1864. She visited that neutral port for a supply of stores and coals and to repair her machinery. Soon after she anchored, a boat came alongside and asked her name. The Confederate gave his reply in all honesty. A person in the boat responded, this boat is from her British Majesty's steamer Curlew. The thing was untrue, for no British man-of-war was in port at that time.

The Florida was discovered, and in a few hours, in the dead of night, her crew were butchered and the vessel towed out of port and taken to Hampton Roads, where we all know how and by whom she was destroyed. That destruction was ordered by the Lincoln Government to avoid an honest

187

restitution, and it found a fellow supple enough to do the work.

It would never have occurred in an English or French port. To build fighting ships abroad was an easy task[44] but to get them to sea and man them was a difficult task. A sailor's devotion while serving in a ship grows, and at mention of her name his heart warms and he is ever ready to defend her honor, hence the restless impatience of the crew of the Alabama to engage the Kearsarge.

What else except the sailor's belief in the life of ships makes the parallel between ships' lives and men's lives so pleasant and constant a fable? As on land, so on sea, you have them of all sorts. There is the national ship, proud, stately, warlike. There is the great merchantman, rich, solid, busy. There is the fat, bustling trader rolling up and down the coast with coals or cattle or produce. There are the graceful, lively, gaily-dressed pleasure crafts, yachts and despatch boats, the ladies of the sea. There are the industrious, disregarded smacks and pungy's, working hard for every inch of luck they get, and taking the weather pretty much as it comes, which nobody counts and nobody cares for. And the reason why a ship's fate affects one so much is always the sailor's reason.

When we see a great vessel rolling lonely at sea, her masts gone, her gear loose and adrift, and sheets of foaming sea pouring in and out of her helpless sides, who wants the fable explained? Many such a craft, once proud and capable, wallows among the screaming seabirds of destiny upon the waters of life. Practical and unimaginative people may say,

[44] Waddell was mistaken here. Bulloch had one of the most difficult assignments his country could give him—to build a navy in foreign ports.

188

what difference does it make to the ship, but no sailor will listen to that.

Imaginative theorists have declared that naval supremacy is due to a pronoun. We call a ship "she" and other tongues call a ship "it." "She" implies that the ship carries us and is in some manner alive, as a sailor in his heart privately believes, or why does he talk about her foot, her waist, her head, her dimity when the graceful thing floats on the surface of the water?

There is life in the craft from the time she leaves the ways into the tide, to the hour when her timbers are laid on the sand or rocks, or, the saddest of all, in the ship-broker's yard.

The worst of the iron plated vessel is that the black, ugly armor has no such vitality and cannot be christened with the pretty old-fashioned names which helped the sailors' superstition out, we cannot answer for such hideous monsters. They are created out of dull mineral which came from the bowels of the earth, and should they not all come to grief like the monitor, the blacksmith will some day turn them into pots and pans, iron railings and boilers. But the timber of the wooden ship grew in sunlight, it waved in the forest and heard the wind sing, before bending to the breeze under topsails.

# APPENDIX

The diplomatic correspondence arising out of the case of the Shenandoah is laid before the public. While France and England took precisely the same course, the Washington Government fawned on and flattered the one while it insulted and menaced the other. When the Government of the United States had proclaimed the blockade of the Southern ports, and thereby recognized, as laid down by their own supreme court, a state of war, they fiercely complained that the English took notice of that state of war and recognized the belligerent character of the Confederacy, without which recognition the English would have been speedily involved in war. They complained that English merchants exercised the neutral right of selling arms and ammunition to the South at the peril of the carriers and this when they themselves were importing guns and gunpowder in enormous quantities.

They complained that Englishmen contrived to enter the service of the South at a time when their own authorities admitted that two-fifths of their own armies were composed of foreigners and when their ships were chiefly manned by English seamen. They were even childish enough to complain that Englishmen sympathised with the South, and cheered and feasted the officers of Southern vessels, with such unmanly and petulant nonsense they interlarded despatches in which they raised complaints that were not so palpably absurd, complaints that Confederate cruisers had

190

escaped from English ports to prey upon their merchant vessels, and that the British Government had failed to do its duty in arresting them.

Any other power might have deserved some sympathy in such a case, even if its complaints were not solidly founded in law. But not so the United States. They had strict legal justice and that was all and more than they deserved at British hands.

Lord Russell was harsh but consistent towards the Confederacy. Louis Napoleon was treacherous and deceived us. During the war of the Spanish colonies, fleets of privateers had issued from American ports to cruise against Spanish commerce, and returning thither had refitted and sold their prizes. And during the Crimean War an American-built cruiser was sent out to Russia and actually protected from the search and seizure on her way by an American squadron.

With these precedents in their memory, it is wonderful the Americans dared to make any complaints. Yet they went so far as to threaten the British with a piratical attack upon their ports if they allowed the Confederate vessels the reception which neutrality obliged them to accord.

They denounced all the Confederate cruisers indiscriminately, those which took their departure from Confederate ports, like the Florida, Sumter, Tallahassee, and those which were armed on the high seas, like the Alabama, Shenandoah, and the Georgia as pirates. And while making no vigorous attempt to capture them, pretended to hold England responsible for what was achieved under the Confederate flag by ships that had no connection with England save that of being built by Englishmen.

The last letter to which Lord Clarendon replied is one from Mr. Seward communicated to Mr. Adams. It intimates that the Federal Government were aware that no application for the surrender of the crew of the Shenandoah would be attended by that of England and proceeds to complain that the crew and captain of the Shenandoah were not tried for piracy.

He observes that Lord Russell chose to accept the "prevaricating statement" of the captain as clearing him from that charge, whereas the piratical acts complained of were committed in British ports, and the men who could prove them, i.e., the sailors on board the Shenandoah, were in British custody.

Now if this means anything, it means that the charge of piracy on which the English Government ought to have tried the men, and which was committed in British ports, was that to which my plea referred.

Now I had confined myself entirely to the real question of piracy, the continuance of capture after the war was over, the latter part of Mr. Seward's assertion is utterly irrelevant and inapplicable and is not clear why he chose to write a thing so foolishly absurd.

Only by a strained interpretation was it possible to put any sense on Mr. Seward's words save one, plainly, ridiculously, and knowingly false, and his man Friday, Charles Francis Adams, was in no better condition of mind or tongue, and Lord Clarendon strained the point accordingly.

He separates the two closely connected sentences the "prevaricating plea of the captain" and the refuting evidence in British custody, and supposes the one to refer to the real, the other to the constructive charge of piracy. For the term pirate is applicable to the Shenandoah in these different senses.

First as to the Sumter merely as a term of abuse, meaning that she was a vessel whose exploits had put the Federal Government in a childish passion. Next, as applicable to her conduct from the 26th of June to the 2nd of August, third as implying that she was not a ship of war, but a British merchantman.

After sharply rebuking the insolent insinuation that justice was not to be obtained from the British Government, Lord Clarendon proceeds to dispose of the two last points.

First, he could not try Captain Waddell as a pirate for having continued his voyage after being informed of the cessation of war. His first intimation of General Lee's surrender is said by witnesses produced by the American minister to have been received on the 26th of June.

The evidence produced is little better than hearsay. It comes from a man who, having served on board the Shenandoah and since turned informer, is entitled to no credit, and if admitted and believed, it proves only that a report on which I was in no way bound to act, of a fact which did not imply the cessation of hostilities, was made to me by a prisoner.

There is no reason to believe that I ever received or did receive any credible news even of General Lee's surrender till the second day of August, when I instantly put the guns in the hold and sailed for Liverpool. Secondly, as it is perfectly certain that the Shenandoah was transferred to the Confederate Government before she fired a gun or started on a cruise, it was impossible to prosecute her captain or the crew on the other ground alleged by Mr. Adams, and it may be observed that if the Shenandoah had remained technically an English ship, still having a commission from the Confederate Government, she would have been, not a pirate, but a privateer.

The truth is, England did everything that neutrality permitted to aid the stronger belligerent, and it is well for her peace of mind that the battle was given to the strong. She might have found it very difficult to answer a Confederate remonstrance against her repeated manifestations of partiality to Northern interest.

The British Government surrendered the Shenandoah to the United States Government on the claim that she was the property of the late Confederate States (what becomes of the charge of piracy?) and the Government of the United States sold her to an English company, and finally the Sultan of Zanzibar bought her for his pleasure yacht.

Some years after she was on her way to Bombay and encountering a gale went down with all on board off the Island of Socotra, except one or more persons who were picked up by a passing vessel who told her end.[45]

[45] See Prefatory Note for the story of the tragic end of the *Shenandoah.*

# Prizes Captured by the Confederate
# S.S. Shenandoah

Following is a list of the ships captured, burned, and ransomed by the *Shenandoah,* which appeared as an appendix in Lieutenant C. Hunt's book, *The Shenandoah or the Last Confederate Cruiser,* published in London and New York simultaneously in 1866.

There are some minor discrepancies between Hunt's list, Waddell's memoirs, a list compiled by John Bigelow when he was preparing his *France and the Confederate Navy,* published in 1871, and Surgeon Lining's and Midshipman Mason's journals. For example, Hunt and Waddell differ as to the dates when some of the ships were captured, the spelling of the names of three of the vessels, and, on one occasion, the number of prisoners taken. Bigelow's list follows the one in Hunt's book, which he undoubtedly used in his research. The journals of Surgeon Lining and Midshipman Mason also follow Hunt's list closely in dates and spelling.

I cross-checked the five sources with the official list of the *Shenandoah's* captures included in the minutes of the Alabama Claims Commission hearings. This list compares favorably with Hunt's with one exception—the United States attorneys included three ships not on any other list!

I finally decided to use Hunt's list because it was published within a year after the *Shenandoah's* cruise, whereas Waddell wrote his memoirs twenty-one years later when he was an old man and a year from the grave. Although they added three more ships to Hunt's list, the government attorneys apparently accepted his account of the cruise as accurate; it is frequently quoted as evidence in the government's lengthy brief against Great Britain in the Commission's hearings.

However, all the discrepancies are minor. Waddell, Hunt, Bigelow, Lining and Mason, and even the government's dry legal phraseology all agree on the one important point—the *Shenandoah* did inflict tremendous damage on the Merchant Marine of the United States.

The letters "N.B." are believed to mean "No Bond."

Barque Alina of Searsport, lat. 15°25′ N., long. 26°44′ W., value $95,000, captured Oct. 30, from Newport bound to Buenos Ayres [*sic*], 12 persons.

Schooner Charter Oak, San Francisco, lat. 7°38′ N., long. 27°49′ W., value $15,000, captured Nov. 5, from Boston to San Francisco, 9 persons.

Barque D. Godfrey, Boston, lat. 4°42′ N., long. 28°24′ W., value $36,000, captured Nov. 8, from Boston to Valparaiso, 12 persons.

Brig Susan, New York, lat. 4°24′ N., long. 26°39′ W., value $5,436, captured Nov. 10, from Cardiff to Rio Grande, 6 persons.

S. ship Kate Prince, Portsmouth, N. J., lat. 1°45′ N., long. 29°22′ W., rsmd. $40,000, captured Nov. 12, from Cardiff to Bahia, S. A., 20 persons.

Schooner L. M. Stacey, Boston, lat. 1°40′ N., long. 28°24′ W., value $15,000, captured Nov. 13, from Boston to Sandwich Islands, 6 persons.

Barque Edward, whaler, N. B., lat. 37°47′ S., long 12°30′30″ W., value $20,000, captured Dec. 4, from N. Bedford to whaling, 25 persons.

Barque Delphine, Bangor, Me., lat. 39°13′ S., long. 68°33′ E., value $25,000, captured Dec. 29, from London to Akyab, 17 persons.

Barque Adelaide, Baltimore, lat. 1°45′ N., long. 29°22′ W., B., cargo $24,000, from Baltimore to Rio, 15 persons.

Barque Pearl, New London, Ascension Island, value $10,000, captured April 1, whaling.

Edward Carey, San Francisco, Ascension Island, value $15,000, captured April 1, whaling.

Ship Hector, New Bedford, Ascension Island, value $58,000, captured April 1, whaling.

Barque Harvest, Honolulu, Ascension Island, value $34,759, captured April 1, whaling.

(Combined persons on last four ships: 130)

Barque Abigail, New Bedford, Ochotsk [Okhotsk] Sea, value $16,705, captured May 27, whaling, 36 persons.

Ship William Thompson, New Bedford, off Cape Thadevus, value $40,925, captured June 22, whaling, 35 persons.

Ship Euphrates, New Bedford, off Cape Thadevus, value $42,320, captured June 22, whaling, 35 persons.

Barque William C. Nye, New Bedford, near Behring Straits, value $31,512, captured June 25, whaling, 35 persons.

Ship Sophia Thornton, New Bedford, near Behring Straits, value $70,000, captured June 22, whaling, 35 persons.

Barque Nimrod, New Bedford, near Behring Straits, value $29,260, captured June 25, whaling, 35 persons.

Barque Catherine, New Bedford, near Behring Straits, value $26,174 captured June 25, whaling, 35 persons.

Barque Gypsey, New Bedford, near Behring Straits, value, $34,369, captured June 25, whaling.

Barque Isabella, New Bedford, near Behring Straits, value $38,000, June 25, whaling, 3 persons.

Barque General Pike, New Bedford, near Behring Straits, value R. $30,000, June 25 captured, whaling, 35 persons.

Barque Favorite, Fairhaven, near Behring Straits, value $57,896, captured June 28, whaling, 35 persons.

Barque General Williams, N. B., Behring Straits, value $44,750, captured June 25, whaling, 35 persons.

Barque Congress, N. B., near Behring Straits, value $55,300, captured June 28, whaling, 35 persons.

Barque Hillman, N. B., near Behring Straits, value $33,000, captured June 28, whaling, 35 persons.

Ship Isaac Howland, N. B., near Behring Straits, value $75,112, captured June 28, whaling, 35 persons.

Brig Susan Abigail, N. B., near Behring Straits, value $6,500, captured June 25, whaling, 20 persons.

Ship Nassau, N. B., near Behring Straits, value $40,000, captured June 28, whaling, 35 persons.

Barque Martha, N. B., Behring Straits, value $30,307, captured June 28, whaling, 35 persons.

Barque Waverly, N. B., Behring Straits, value $62,376, captured June 28, whaling, 35 persons.

Barque Covington, N. B., value $30,000, captured June 28, whaling, 35 persons.

Barque Jiveh Swift, N. B., near Behring Straits, value $61,960, captured June 22, whaling, 35 persons.

Ship Brunswick, N. B., near Behring Straits, value $16,272, captured June 28, whaling, 35 persons.

Ship James Murry, near Behring Straits, R. $40,550, captured June 28, whaling, 35 persons.

Ship Milo, R. $30,000, captured June 28, whaling, 35.

Barque Nile, New London, R. $25,550, captured June 28, whaling, 35 persons.

Total No. of persons, 1,053.

# BIBLIOGRAPHY

ADAMS, BROOKS, "The Seizure of the Laird Rams," *Proceedings of the Massachusetts Historical Society*, XLV.

*The Alabama Claims Commission; the Case of the United States Against Great Britain.*

BIGELOW, JOHN, *France and the Confederate States Navy.*

BULLOCH, JAMES D., *Secret Service of the Confederate States in Europe or How the Confederate Cruisers were Equipped.* 2 vols. London, 1883.

CALLAHAN, J. M., *The Diplomatic History of the Southern Confederacy.*

———, "James Dunwoody Bulloch," *Dictionary of American Biography*, III.

*Case Presented on Part of the Government of Her Brittanic Majesty, to the Tribunal of Arbitration*, House, Ex. Cocs., 42 Congress, 2 session. No. 282. (Ser. Nos. 1517-1519.) 3 vols. Washington, 1872.

*The Cases of the United States to be Laid Before the Tribunals of Arbitration to be Convened at Geneva.*

*The Confederate Cruiser Shenandoah and the Geneva Awards.*

*The Confederate Veteran*, IX.

*Court of the Commissioners of the Alabama Claims.* (Schedule of Vessels Named in the Claims in Court of 1874.)

*Cruise of the Shenandoah, Insurance Claims and the Geneva Award.*

*Foreign Relations of the United States*, Washington, 1862.

GRIMBALL, JOHN, "Cruise of the Shenandoah," *Southern Historical Society Papers*, Vol. 25, 1897.

HACKETT, FRANK WARREN, *Reminiscences of the Geneva Tribunal.*

HENDRICK, BURTON J., *Statesmen of the Lost Cause.*

HILL, JIM DAN, *Sea Dogs of the Sixties.*

HORN, STANLEY F., *The Gallant Rebel, the Fabulous Cruise of the Shenandoah.*

HUNT, C. E., *The Shenandoah or the Last Confederate Cruiser.*

JOURDAN, D., and PRATT, E. J., *Europe and the American Civil War.*

"The Journal of Charles E. Lining," *A Calendar of Confederate Papers Prepared under the direction of the Confederate Memorial Literary Society.* Richmond, Virginia, 1908.

KNIGHT, L. L. *Georgia Landmarks, Memorials and Legends,* Vol. II.

LINING, DR. CHARLES, "Cruise of the Confederate Shenandoah," *Tennessee Historical Magazine,* Vol. 8, 1924.

MAYNARD, DOUGLAS H., "Plotting the Escape of the Alabama," *The Journal of Southern History,* May, 1954.

————, "Union Attempts to Prevent the Escape of the Alabama," *Mississippi Valley Historical Review,* June, 1954.

*Message of the President of the United States in Answer to a Resolution Passed by the House of Representatives,* Washington, 1866.

MORGAN, MURRAY C., *Dixie Raider.*

OWSLEY, FRANK LAURENS, *King Cotton Diplomacy.*

*Papers Relating to the Treaty of Washington,* Vol. I.

*The Rebel Pirate Shenandoah,* U.S. Naval Affairs, House Document 35.

ROBERTS, WILLIAM P., "James Dunwoody Bulloch and the Confederate Navy," *The North Carolina Historical Review,* July, 1947.

SCOTT, ERNEST, "The Shenandoah Incident," *Victorian Historical Society Magazine,* London, 1926.

WALL, SARAH AGNES, and GILLESPIE, FRANCES EMMA (eds.), *The Journals of Benjamin Moran, 1857-1865.* 2 vols.

WHITTLE, WILLIAM C., "Cruise of the Shenandoah," *Southern Historical Papers,* Vol. 35, 1907.

200